Inspire!
Writing from the Soul
Linda C. Apple

AWOC.COM Publishing
Denton Texas

AWOC.COM Publishing
P.O. Box 2819
Denton, TX 76202

© 2009 by Linda C. Apple
All Rights Reserved.

No part of this publication may be reproduced, stored in a retrieval system, or transmitted in any form or by any means, electronic, mechanical, recording or otherwise, without written permission, except in the case of brief quotations embodied in critical articles and reviews.

Manufactured in the United States of America

ISBN: 978-0-937660-79-9

Revised

Visit Linda C. Apple's web site: www.LindaCApple.com

Dedication

To my husband, Neal Apple.

You are my soulmate and kindred spirit. I have been blessed by your generous spirit and servant's heart for over thirty years and especially appreciate your support during this project.

Thank you for taking my car keys away so I would write, for cooking and cleaning on the weekends and listening to me think outloud.

You inspire me. I love you.

A Special Thank You To

My family. Thank you for your love, support, and encouragement. You patiently listened to what I wrote and the many rewrites. Thank you for not writing sarcastic notes on the dusty furniture or complaining about leftovers. I promise a big family dinner soon.

Velda Brotherton, my friend and mentor. Thank you for taking time from your writing to sharpen mine. Your prose is poetry and your beautiful spirit infuses everything you write. You have been a blessing to my life.

Dusty Richards and the Northwest Arkansas Writers Workshop. Thank you, friends, for creating an atmosphere where success is celebrated and failure isn't the end of the world. When I fail, you pick me up, dust me off, and give me the shove I need to keep moving forward.

Dan Case, publisher, editor, and all around great guy. He is the visionary for this book. Thank you, Dan for giving me this splendid opportunity to encourage others to inspire.

Above all, I give thanks to the Lord Jesus Christ. He gives me life, eternal perspective, hope, and purpose. Even in life's shadowy valleys of death, He is with me, leading me to the light.

Table of Contents

Foreword 9
Introduction 11
Reflecting 15
   What Is Inspirational Writing? 16
      The Passion, Purpose, and Power 17
      Reaching Through the Generations 18
      The Difference 18
   Inspirational Writing Begins With You 21
   The Market 25
      Inspirational Fiction 25
      Anthologies 25
      Magazines 26
      Newspapers 27
      Devotionals 28
      Do Your Homework 29
   Getting Ideas 30
      Pictures 30
      Free writing 30
      Lists 31
      Quotes 31
      Reading 32
Write! 33
   Consider 34
   Connect 35
   Compose 38
      Setting a Scene 40
      Using an Anchor 40
      The Purpose of Scenes and Anchors 41
      Description 44
      Reclaim Wonder 50
      Emotion 56
      Dialogue 68
      Internalization 72
      Our Gift 76
      Practice, Practice, Practice 79

Write Right 84
   Words! Keep them simple 84
   Vivid Nouns 85
   Keep them active 86
   Adverb Fatigue 87
   Raving Repetition 90
   Tricky Words 93
   Homophone Imposters 94
   Punctuation 98
   Laying Our Words on the Sacrificial Altar .. 103
Inspire! 107
   A City on a Hill or a Candle Under a Bowl? ... 108
   Rejection letters 108
   Tackling Our Writing Demons 109
   I'm a Nobody 112
   Who Cares? 113
   It All Counts–My Soapbox 114
   Write! 119

Foreword

The inspirational stories and exercises in this book are not limited to writers, but to everyone searching for hidden meanings in their lives. Here Linda openly shares her heartaches and joys in order to help others through difficulties and show them the way to healing through writing.

She is not only a talented writer but an inspirational speaker whose words have long helped others face problems of the heart and soul. With this book, she reaches out to so many who have not had the privilege of knowing her or hearing her speak. Her words of encouragement point the way toward a fuller life and an unending relationship with God.

Following each personal revelation, in what Linda refers to as Sparks, she questions, then prods the reader/writer toward forgotten memories which will inspire and enrich. Step by step, her words become keys to open long ago experiences and relate them to their writing.

Not only does she ignite the heart and soul, she shares her own experiences and how she has dealt with them. The loss of her home, the near death of her son, a questioning of her faith, are all catalysts that built the indomitable spirit with which she faces life today. And all these she shares with the reader, while also encouraging them to accomplish the same.

To read her words is to discover a new strength, and the courage to pick up pen and paper and begin to write. Everyone has a story, and this book will guide them in sharing that story which could well bring solace to others, just as Linda has done.

According to her own words, writers can literally change the course of someone's life through the written word. Writing, she poses, has an eternal quality. Words live forever. In writing *Inspire*, Linda creates a memorable book that is much more than a workbook for writers. It is an inspirational tool for everyone who has ever had a desire to share their own heartaches, strengths and courage with others.

Velda Brotherton —
Author of *Fly with the Mourning Dove*

Introduction

To do something, however small, to make others happier and better, is the highest ambition, the most elevating hope, which can inspire a human being.
—John Lubbock

There is a flame inside every writer, a passion for words, for expression. Mine began as a spark in 1971 in creative writing class. I sat on the second row, third seat down. Mary Steenburgen sat on the first row, second seat.

No kidding! Even then I knew she was special.

Me? Plain vanilla in a cardboard-tasting cone.

That is, until my teacher, Ms. Emily Kelso, ignited a spark within my soul. She opened the world of prose. She taught me how to use words and express the things I didn't have courage to say out loud. I learned to reach deep and discovered, well, myself.

On the last day of class I asked her to sign my yearbook. That's when it happened. With the strike of her pen on paper she wrote, "To Linda, One day you will be a great writer," and the spark glowed into a flame.

Emily inspired me.

After high school I went to college and continued to write. However, in the first year I got my M.R.S. degree and put my pen down—temporarily of course. Nineteen months later I gave birth to a beautiful baby girl. Three months later my husband left.

Devastation made me forget writing all together, if only I'd known the healing properties of writing. Thankfully, mercy blessed us with a man who loved and wanted us both, Neal Apple. Two months after we were married he adopted Amanda and that same week we discovered Rob was on the way. When Rob was nine-months-old we learned that Charles was on the way. Two years after Charles I had Olivia and two years after her came William.

Writing? What's that?

Not only did my large family keep me from writing but life flung a few "curve balls" too. In 1995 our house burned down. Then in 1997 William suffered a brain empyema resulting from a sinus infection that had crossed the blood-brain barrier and infected his right front lobe. We almost lost him. During this time all my high aspirations of raising the perfect Christian children disintegrated in the throes of rebellion. This just wasn't supposed to happen.

The flame died—or so I thought.

In 1998, my now departed friend, Lois Spoon, started a writing group and invited me to come.

Why not? I decided to give it a shot.

The group turned out to be the therapy I needed. Once again, just as Emily had taught me in creative writing, I reached deep and wrote.

A spark ignited but regret kept it from catching fire. After all, I was deep in middle-age. All those years—wasted. Still, I wrote. I wrote about my divorce, a second chance at love, family, and loss. From those stories came epiphanies like how to forgive the man who hurt me and to treasure the man who loved me and our children. After the fire, I learned that stuff is just that—stuff. Nothing I own adds to my self-worth, makes me better or more important. And to my surprise most of my stories about raising teenagers, even though I spent many sleepless, tear-filled, nights, turned out humorous. In fact, a book came from that experience that will be available soon titled, *NOW WHAT DO I DO? Help for When Teenagers Become*

Teenstrangers. It is for Christian parents who raised their children right but these kids still chose wrong.

All those years were not wasted after all. I'd been collecting experiences, learning lessons, maturing into a person who not only expressed my opinions but listened to others.

As I wrote I discovered my voice—the writer's style and unique qualities. It was comfortable, conversational, and encouraging.

Without realizing it, I became an inspirational writer. My fondness for people and the desire to turn my trials into blessings for others flavored everything I wrote. I sold my first story to *Chicken Soup for the Nurses Soul* in 2000 and this story was reprinted in *Woman's World Magazine*. I was in writer's heaven! Then I sold another story to *Chicken Soup for the Working Woman's Soul* in 2002 which was reprinted in the *10th Anniversary Special Edition of Chicken Soup for the Soul Living Your Dreams*.

Riding on this wonderful experience I attended the Ozarks Creative Writer's Conference in Eureka Springs, Arkansas. The first night a woman across the room caught my attention. She was absolutely striking.

The next night we met and she stared at me a moment and then said, "I know you. I taught you in high school."

"That's impossible, you are too young." I knew what I was talking about because all my teachers were dead with old age, or so I perceived.

"I taught you in creative writing."

"Ms. Kelso?" I couldn't believe it. She was *my* age, or very close. We caught up on each other's lives and went into the awards banquet. Fortunately, I won a first place award and in the dark room I heard Emily shout, "I taught her writing!"

That she did and so much more.

I've sold a total of nine stories to *Chicken Soup for the Soul* series. My devotions are published in devotional magazines and anthologies. I've even sold three short-stories. But being published isn't the only thing that thrills me about writing. It is the email I receive from people who express how my writing has helped them—people from all over the world, individuals I will never meet on this side of Heaven.

It just doesn't get better than that!

Do you feel the same way? If so, then inspirational writing may be your genre.

Inspire! Writing from the Soul is written with this goal in mind—to inspire you to inspire others. In it I focus on writing nonfiction articles and books. However, the principles presented in the book can also be applied to inspirational fiction.

This book is meant to be used as an interactive tool. There are exercise prompts throughout. Where you see "**Spark!**" it is your turn to draw from deep within and kindle the flame of inspiration that lives in your soul.

Feed the flame of creativity inside you. Don't smother it or let others snuff it out. Let the glow from your flame warm all who read your words.

Inspire! Write from your soul.

Linda C. Apple—2009

Reflecting

There are two ways of spreading light: to be the candle or the mirror that reflects it. —Edith Wharton, Vesalius in Zante

What Is Inspirational Writing?

In the long history of the world, only a few generations have been granted the role of defending freedom in its hour of maximum danger. I do not shrink from this responsibility—I welcome it. I do not believe that any of us would exchange places with any other people or any other generation. The energy, the faith, the devotion which we bring to this endeavor will light our country and all who serve it—and the glow from that fire can truly light the world.

And so, my fellow Americans: ask not what your country can do for you—ask what you can do for your country.

My fellow citizens of the world: ask not what America will do for you, but what together we can do for the freedom of man. —John F Kennedy

When President Kennedy gave his inaugural address on that cold January day in 1961, I was only six-years-old. I can't remember if I heard him speak that day, but forty plus years later those written words still bring tears to my eyes. They inspire me. Inspire comes from the Latin, *inspirare,* and it means "to breathe upon or into." Merriam-Webster's definition is: to infuse with breath, with life, to produce or arouse a feeling or a thought, to influence or impel, to communicate or suggest by a divine or supernatural influence.

People from all walks of life want and need hope, guidance, encouragement, or just a good laugh. As it says in Proverbs, "a merry heart is good medicine." When we think of "inspirational" writing "religious" comes to mind. While that is a large part of the market, there is a growing trend for this genre in the general market. A great example is the *Chicken Soup for the Soul* books by Jack Canfield and Mark Victor Hanson.

What makes writing inspirational? It is the passion, the purpose, and the motivation of the writer who overcame and learned from adversity and misfortune, then wrote with the desire to help others.

The Passion, Purpose, and Power

Mark Twain wrote: "A drop of ink may make a million think." Throughout history we have witnessed the truth of that statement. Writers carry powerful influence. We can literally change the course of someone's life through the written word.

Harriet Beecher Stowe wrote *Uncle Tom's Cabin* in angry response to the 1850 passage of the Fugitive Slave Act, which punished those who aided runaway slaves and diminished the rights of fugitive slaves as well as freed slaves. It was originally published as a forty week serial. This book has been attributed to raising public awareness and inflaming their passionate disdain. So much so that when Abraham Lincoln met Stowe after the beginning of the Civil War, he said to her, "so you're the little lady whose book started this great war."

Upton Sinclair wrote *The Jungle* after an assignment to write a journalistic expose on the Chicago stockyards. He was appalled at the illegal practices and unsanitary food handling. No publisher would touch this book so Sinclair self-published it. The public, including President Theodore Roosevelt, reacted with unmitigated horror. After reading *The Jungle*, he ordered an immediate investigation into the meat industry that resulted in "The Pure Food and Drug Act" and the "Meat Inspection Act." Sinclair reportedly said, "I aimed at the public's heart and by accident I hit it in the stomach."

True writers are driven by passion and purpose. Whether we realize it or not, what is important to us is evident in our work. Stowe appealed to society's sense of fairness and compassion. Sinclair exposed what was being done in secret. Both inspired change. Little did they know the world-wide impact they would have or how the course of history for future generations would be altered for the better.

Reaching Through the Generations

Like no other medium, writing has an eternal quality. Words on paper can have a ripple affect on future generations. Anne Frank, a Jewish teenager during the Nazi German occupation, went into hiding with her family for two years in secret rooms in her father's office. While there, she wrote in her diary:

"I know that I'm a woman, a woman with inner strength and a great deal of courage. If God lets me live, I'll achieve more than Mother ever did. I'll make my voice heard. I'll go out into the world and work for humanity."

Four months after writing that in her diary, she and her family were discovered and taken to a concentration camp. Seven months later she died of typhus. But death did not end her goal. She did achieve more than her mother. Her voice was heard. She posthumously worked for humanity. How? By her writing. That's the power of a drop of ink.

The Difference

As with most people, life has presented many hardships. I've been divorced, my house burned down, my child almost died, and I've survived five teenagers.

When hardships came my way I had a choice—either let them darken me or deepen me. Think of a painting. It is the shading—the shadows—that give the picture depth and dimension. Shading correctly applied makes the painting a beautiful masterpiece. So it is with the dark times of our lives. If we regard our trials in a constructive light and learn from them, our characters are deepened.

After I finally overcome and learn from adversity, my natural inclination is to help others in the same situation. As my friend and pastor, Steve Dixon, says, "No one can help someone like someone who's been there."

When I joined Lois' writing group, my writing, fiction and nonfiction, stemmed from my past experiences and my passion to connect. I wanted to help those who read my stories. That is what drives me. Whether I'm having coffee with someone or speaking at a conference, my purpose is to improve their lives.

Inspirational writers' experiences with pain and tragedy drive them to give hope to those who are trying to survive the same waves of sorrow.

Horatio G. Spafford penned the words to the well known hymn, *It is Well with My Soul*, after learning that his four daughters had drowned. He and his family were going to Europe on a vacation when, at the last minute, business kept him stateside. Horatio sent his family ahead promising to join them later. Just a little before 2:00 a.m. November 22, 1873 their steamship, *Ville du Havre*, collided with the Scottish iron clipper, *Loch Earn*. The ship sunk in 12 minutes. Mrs. Spafford survived and upon arriving in England she sent a telegram to her husband, "Saved alone. What shall I do?"

While crossing the ocean to his wife, the captain of the ship told him when they were in the vicinity of his daughters' watery grave. That night in his cabin he wrote these words:

> *When peace, like a river, attendeth my way,*
> *when sorrows like sea billows roll;*
> *whatever my lot, thou hast taught me to say,*
> *It is well, it is well with my soul.*
> *It is well with my soul,*
> *it is well, it is well with my soul.*

All stanzas of this song offer eternal perspective and hope. Even through his pain he penned these words. That is what inspirational writers do naturally.

They write with the reader in mind. Before I begin any article I ask myself, "What do I want my reader to take away from this? What is my gift to them?" With that goal firmly in my thoughts I begin to write. I may not make an overt statement of my goal, but it flavors my article like salt enhances food.

The unique aspect of this genre is that it has a message that often encompasses overcoming difficult struggles or choices. Some offer a new point of view, while others bring a smile to the readers face. Whatever the subject matter, even in controversial articles, there is always a positive, uplifting end that contains an observation, an epiphany or simple lesson.

The greatest gift we can give through our words on paper or the Internet is hope—a flame in the darkness to help others find their way.

> *You must be the change you wish to see in the world.* —Mahatma Gandhi

Inspirational Writing Begins With You

Who are you, really? Years ago at a conference, Page Lambert, author of *In Search of Kinship*, spoke about the landscape of our lives and how they shape who we are, what we are, and why we think the way we do. Then she made a most profound statement, "We cannot change the pain of the past, but we can give health to the future."

To discover my "landscape," I made a list of the influential people and events in my life. Then I made a separate sheet for each item on the list. For the next few days I spent time writing all the things that came to my mind on each sheet. Memories long forgotten came to the surface. For example my grandmother's sheet:

> *Mammie: adored me, walked a million miles with me in the zoo, bought my first banana split, I miss her, rode the bus with her to work, Krystal hamburgers, had beautiful gardens, played in the yard sprinkler while she weeded, had tea parties under the magnolia tree...*

The list was much longer, but you get the idea. From that list I wrote a story titled, *Digging in the Dirt* and sold it to *Chicken Soup for the Grandma's Soul*. Note how that list inspired my story:

DIGGING IN THE DIRT

"Dig in the dirt with me, Noni."

My three-year-old grandson, Ethan, stood in the kitchen with pleading eyes and a large spoon.

Earlier in the day my daughter had dropped him off on her way to the hair salon. As usual, I was busy and wondered what I could do to keep him occupied? Then I remembered that I had two large clay pots with soil that needed changing. He needed something to do—a perfect solution. I gave him the necessary digging utensils from my junk drawer and told him to dig in the dirt. He rushed to the deck and sent potting soil flying everywhere. I could just imagine my daughter's reaction to his dirty clothes, but that was okay with me. I'm the grandma and I'm allowed to spoil.

Now, he wanted a playmate. It was hard to resist his invitation, but I was in a rush trying to cook supper so I could go to a meeting later that evening.

"I can't right now, Honey. Noni's busy."

He hung his head and stared at his shoes on his way back to the deck. Guilt hovered over me while I chopped celery and onions for meatloaf.

Some grandma!

My mental scolding turned to reasoning. It's different being a grandparent these days, I'm younger, busier. I don't have time to play like my grandmother, whom I'd named Mammie, did when I was a child.

I watched Ethan through the window and remembered all the tea parties Mammie and I had. She filled my blue, plastic teapot with coffee-milk—more milk and sugar than coffee. Then she'd toast pound cake and slather it with butter. We sat under the old magnolia tree in the back yard. I served the cake and poured the coffee into tiny, robin-egg blue cups and stirred with an even tinier spoon. Our play time probably lasted less than thirty minutes, and yet, after all these years I still treasured our times together. Her smile, her laugh, and the fragrance of those creamy white magnolia blooms have remained with me all these years.

Ethan caught me watching him and pointed to the pot. He had emptied it. I waved and nodded to him. Just then it dawned on me that my love for flowers came from my grandmother because she had taken the time to dig in the dirt with me. What better gift could I give my grandson than memories of love and being loved?

Inside the garage was a new bag of potting soil and packs of flower seeds. What fun it would be to plant seeds and watch them grow with my little grandson. I left my knife on the chopping block, found another old spoon and went to dig in the dirt.

"Noni can play now."

Ethan clapped his earth covered hands as I plopped down beside him. What fun we had that sunny afternoon planting seeds and memories. I discovered the secret that my grandmother had always known—there is always time to play.

After all, grandmothers are just little girls at heart.

Spark!

What is your landscape?

- Make a list of influential people and events in your life since childhood. Good and bad.
- Put each name and event on a separate sheet of paper
- Choose a sheet and write whatever comes to mind for ten minutes per sheet, and don't worry about grammar, just write.
- Do this each day with a different sheet as a writing warm-up.

What is important to you? Ask yourself the following questions and then write *everything* that comes to mind even if it doesn't make sense:

- **What makes me pound the table**? Have you ever been in a conversation and the subject had you pounding the table in an effort to get your point across? In a discussion what do you usually change the subject to? What do you daydream about? To what are you willing to devote your life?

- **What are you interested in?** Make a list of all the things that have held your fascination since childhood. Things you are curious about. Future dreams and hopes.
- **What would you change if you could?** Things you would do different in your life, things you would change in and for your family, friends, people in your city, state, country, or world.
- **If you were given the power to never fail, what kind of things would you do?** In your personal life, in your family and friends, in the world.
- **What do you believe?** About life, love, friendship, integrity, morality, eternity, peace, etc.

You may be surprised at what you remember, or the connections your past has to your present. Hopefully, you will recognize things about yourself that will translate into valuable inspirational articles.

The Market

As I mentioned earlier, the Inspirational Market is wide open for both fiction and nonfiction. The attack on the people of the United States of America on 9/11 changed life as we know it forever. Mistrust burned into the fabric of our beings. Fear clouds us like never before. It has made everyday life more complicated and travel more frustrating than ever. And then there is the uncertain economy.

No wonder people are grasping for good news, help, hope, and encouragement. Let's take a look at market opportunities.

Inspirational Fiction

I once heard a writer say fiction is to writing what anesthesia is to major surgery. Fiction allows the writer to address the more difficult, edgier subjects by way of their characters and storyline.

Fiction provides a safe place for the reader. It is much easier to read about a character being plagued by the same thing that may be troubling his or her own life, like addictions, abuse, hate, fear, or loss.

Author, Linda Hargrove, addressed abuse in her novel, *Loving Cee Cee Johnson*. The reader didn't choose the book because it was about abuse, but because it has a great storyline. Nevertheless, the reader is learning how to recover and to forgive while reading how Cee Cee learned to do the same.

Writer's guidelines for Christian fiction vary. Be sure and check the website of the publishing house you are interested in submitting to and read what they will and will not accept.

Anthologies

An anthology is a collection of stories. Fiction anthologies are made up of short stories. Nonfiction anthologies usually have a theme and the stories published in them are inspirational, personal experience, stories about that theme. The most popular are the *Chicken Soup for the Soul* books published by Health Communications.

Jack Canfield and Mark Victor Hanson, both motivational and inspirational speakers, often used anecdotes about ordinary people doing extraordinary things. After their presentations, people from the audience would ask for a copy of one of the stories to give to a friend or loved one who needed encouragement. Thus, the idea was born.

The title in itself is inspirational. Jack remembered how his grandmother said chicken soup would cure anything. He wanted these books to have the same healing powers for the soul, and that is how the books got their name—by their purpose.

Today there are over two-hundred titles, 112 million copies sold and translated into forty languages.

Publications of this sort are looking for uplifting, positive stories that encourage, and inspire. The endings should show a positive change in someone, or give a simple lesson, or an epiphany. = manifestation of a diety

What they do not want is an essay, (an analytic, speculative, or interpretative composition) a eulogy, (a commendation of praise) anything controversial or political.

It is best to write in the Creative Nonfiction style which is discussed in the *"WRITE!"* section of this book. Also, if possible, keep your word count under the limit. For instance, if the maximum word count allowed is 1200, keep it at 900–1000, or less. Write tight by using strong words.

Magazines

This market offers the greatest variety of writing opportunities. The bad news? It is hard to break into the national market. The best way to start is to go to the magazine you are interested in and check out their website for the writer's guidelines which are usually in the *contact us* section.

Smaller publications are the best place to start. I suggest investing in a *Writer's Market* book, available in most bookstores. It has information on paying markets for magazines, journals, fiction and nonfiction markets. It lists the percentages of freelance articles the publication uses, what kind of articles they are looking for, how much they pay, writing tips, and the contact name–be sure to call and verify the name in case it has changed.

The book is pricey but you can get a better deal on Amazon.com. *Writers Market* is also available as a web-based service and is updated throughout the year plus it offers a community site where you can get advice and tips from other writers. The subscription costs a little more, but is well worth it. Go to www.writersmarket.com for more information.

Sally Stuart's Christian Writer's Market Guide is much like *Writers Market* only it is aimed at Christian writers. Again, go to Amazon.com for the best price.

Subscribe to writing magazines like *Writer's Digest Magazine*. This bi-monthly magazine is helpful for writers at all levels and all genres. The articles are written by established writers who instruct, offer advice, encouragement, and often a good dose of humor. They tell of their struggles and how they overcame. Hmmm, would you say they inspire?

Newspapers

Like magazines, newspapers offer a variety of submission choices. In addition to your local paper, try small regional papers, too. Read a few issues to determine their needs and then contact the appropriate editor.

I know, I know, you are shy. So am I. Once I met a lady who was on an extended stay in England. While there she called the local paper and asked if they would be interested in an article about England from a visitor's point-of-view. They did. In fact, they assigned several more articles to her.

As my friend Lois once told me, "The worst they can do is say no."

Devotionals

This market is primarily religious. That said, books with positive, motivational messages are growing in popularity. In our busy culture it is nice to have a short read in the morning that centers us with a positive frame of mind.

Again, it is best to do the research and find which devotionals accept outside writers—some only use "in house" writers—then go to their website for the guidelines.

Good devotions grow from the scripture. They help the reader better understand the Bible and how to apply it to their life.

They contain an anecdote or personal experience. It needs to be true and should be an accurate reflection of the writer's experience. Use one main point. Focus on one truth, one event, a moment in time. Reflect on everyday events and human experiences.

Use universal themes and images. Subjects like forgiveness, overcoming worry, loving our neighbor. If the publication is worldwide, think about your subject carefully. For instance, pet stories aren't good because some countries may have dogs or cats in the freezer for company dinner. Dieting isn't a good subject either, since most the world would love the opportunity to be fat.

Finally, use a transition to pull the reader from the anecdote to the scripture and show the reader how to apply it.

Never preach. Avoid words like "you." Instead, use "we" or "us." Don't use phrases like "ought to" or "have to," and steer clear of absolutes like "never" or "always."

Devotions are usually less than three-hundred words. For a great example, check out AWOC.COM Publishing's imprint, *Devoted To* series.

Do Your Homework

Choose your markets and study them. Look at the magazines you are interested in and jot down the kinds of articles they publish. Look at the ads. Note the demographics they cater to, for instance, young women, mothers, women over forty? Young men, middle-age, or men with health issues? Also, notice the words that are used in ads. The people who write them make their living at choosing the best words. Use them in your queries. Read the books, devotionals, anthologies and notice their style and what they publish. Study submission guidelines and follow them to the absolute t-crosses and i-dots! And as I mentioned earlier, make sure you use the name of the editor, not "to whom it may concern," and be sure you spell it correctly. Editors are pretty sensitive about that.

Getting Ideas

For some people the ideas flow, for others they freeze on the blank screen. Here are a few ways to thaw out your creativity:

Pictures

Pictures are a great way to unlock memories. Things long forgotten surface along with the emotions, senses, and details that enhance our stories. I decided to send a story about my brother, Kirk, to the *Chicken Soup for the Soul Celebrating Brothers and Sisters*. I stared at the blank screen and it stared back. Neither of us budged. So I gave up and decided to clean the closet. While moving things around I found a box of photographs. There was a photo of Kirk, just before he left for Vietnam. Recollections flooded me, the emotions, the dialogue, the senses. I jotted everything down and wrote my story. A few months after submitting it, they accepted and published it.

Free writing

This technique helps you loosen up, get ideas, and to let go. Choose a topic and write nonstop for a set period of time anything that comes into your mind, even it has nothing to do with the topic. You might have a thought like; I sure could use some chocolate right about now, write it down and keep going. Don't stop to edit or make corrections. Keep moving the pen forward. You can do this at your computer too. Start typing and don't look at the screen. Let your thoughts flow. For example, I'll free write about airline travel:

it used to be exciting but nowit is frustrating and humiliating when the buzzer goes off and ou have to get patted down it makes me angry that it will no longer be like it was when my kids were small and we could watch dad get off the plane and meet him at the gate and there isn't food any morfe, even if it wasn't good at leastg there was something to eatand it scares me theat the planes are betting older too

You know, I didn't plan on writing about frustration, but that is what came out. As you can see, there are typos and unfinished, rambling thoughts. But there is also an article in there.

Lists

Choose a topic and make a list of everything that comes to mind from your past to the present. For example, I'll use the topic "coffee." My list would look like this:

Front porch, humming birds, coffee-milk with grandmother, summer evenings, friends, Barnes and Noble, long talks, welcome, comfort.

My list may look strange to you, but these are the thoughts that came to me because on warm days I enjoy sipping coffee on the front porch and watching the hummers fight over sugar water. When I was a girl my grandmother made me coffee-milk in the mornings. Summer evenings I enjoy coffee while watching the sunset and the fireflies begin their dance. Then there are the coffee-klatches with friends at my favorite place. When I enter a home, the aroma of coffee says, "welcome" or if a friend comes to my home distressed about something, the steaming mug brings comfort.

From the above paragraph many stories could be told.

Quotes

As you can tell, I'm a quote fanatic. They jog my creativity like nothing else can. Search "quotes" and enjoy reading. Something will strike a note with you. My favorite quote site is: www.thinkexist.com.

Reading

Good writers write. Great writers read. Always read with your journal and pen close by. See how other writers express themselves, notice their style. Write what you learn from them and any inspiring thoughts they spark.

> **Spark!**
> Build an inspirational story as you read this book.

Throughout the book I will give an **I.S.~Spark!** (Inspirational Story) prompt. By the time you reach the end, you will have a great start on something to submit.

Start by choosing a photo from your family album, study it a moment and then free write everything that comes to your mind for ten minutes.

Read what you wrote and choose a couple of themes that would make a good personal experience story

Write them down on separate sheets of paper and list everything that comes to mind concerning that theme. This exercise will help focus your story. Write for ten minutes.

At the top of the journal page, give this theme a "working title." It is called that because you or your publisher may change the title later.

Decide on at least two markets where you would like to submit your inspirational story and write those down on your paper.

Write!

I am a little pencil in the hand of a writing God who is sending a love letter to the world. —Mother Teresa

Consider

Before you start your article or book, ask yourself, *What is my purpose in writing this? What kind of result am I hoping for? What do I want my reader to glean from my writing?* That is your gift to your reader.

Although you will not write the answers to the above questions in your article, having them firmly in your mind will help you stay focused.

My story, "Connected by Love," in *Chicken Soup for the Father and Daughter Soul* is about my relationship with my step-father who raised me. Even though we do not share the same DNA, people comment how much alike we are in personality and appearance.

My goal was for those who are in adopted or blended family homes to know that it didn't matter if the same blood didn't flow through their veins, the family bond can be just as strong. Having that firmly in mind guided me in writing the article. Before writing your article or book, jot down on an index card or sheet of paper an answer to one, two, or all three goals:

My purpose for writing this
The results I want to have
The gift I'm giving my reader

I.S.~Spark!

Assign at least one goal to your story and write it down.

Connect

Your writing style is a connection point. It should be "conversational." Imagine your reader sitting across the table from you in a coffee shop. The reason you are there is to help this person who is hurting, confused, and just plain discouraged. How would you talk to them? Hopefully, you would speak to them in an easy and friendly manner with a lot of encouragement sprinkled in for good measure.

Another connection point is to tell *enough* of your story in order for your reader to trust that you understand. **Don't overdo it.** I emphasize this because it is a real temptation to write every tiny detail and nuance of our pain, because we think they need to know to appreciate our experience.

I had a dear friend who died of cancer a few years ago. She fought this horrible disease and won the first round. Wanting to encourage others, she compiled several stories of how God helped her in mysterious and wonderful ways. It was marvelous. In fact, a large Christian publishing house was interested in it.

However, in the beginning of the book she wrote, in shocking detail, her experience with her mother's cancer and then her's. It was graphic and disgusting. I advised her to omit these two chapters, but she insisted it was necessary for the reader to understand what she went through. The publishing house asked her to cut them too, but she refused and they rejected it.

We talked about the rejection, and I once again recommended she leave out those chapters. She insisted they stay. I asked, "Would you have wanted to read that when you first learned you had cancer?" She thought a minute and then said, "No."

That didn't make sense to me and I blurted out, "Then why are you asking your reader to?"

Finally, she relented and toned it down—a little. The publishing house rejected her manuscript again. Ultimately a friend who owned a small publishing company published it for her.

I loved and admired my friend, but I still can't in good conscious give her book to anyone who has recently received the diagnosis of cancer. It's a shame because the rest of it is so inspirational. The book is out of print now.

A year after she died I heard an editor speak at a writers conference. He told about an experience at a different conference where a woman attendee approached him and asked if he would read her manuscript. He agreed and took it to his room. The editor said she was an excellent writer, but by the time he finished it he was depressed. The pages were filled with explicit details about the crash, the injuries, the emotional trauma, and her guilt over her daughter's death.

The next morning he met with the woman and complimented her writing style, but told her the manuscript left him feeling depressed and hopeless. He couldn't use it.

Her answer was like my friend's. "But that is what happened. I want people to know what I went through."

An idea came to the editor and he said, "Tell me, did anyone help you during this time?"

"Oh yes," she replied. "My friends and church family brought food, cleaned my house, and drove me to my doctor appointments. Some even stayed with me overnight. They listened when I needed to talk and didn't force me to when I didn't feel like it."

"How did you deal with the guilt?"

"I got counseling and joined support groups."

"That," said the editor, "is what you need to write. Your readers already understand pain. Some of them are in the very throes of it. Take their hand and show them the way to recovery, give them hope."

The woman took his advice and rewrote her book with her reader in mind and he accepted it for publication. The next year, at the same conference, she approached him, beaming.

"I have something else for you to read," she said and handed him a large manila envelope. It was full of letters from bereaved parents from all over the country, thanking her for giving them hope in the darkest hours of their lives.

This woman got it. She understood how to serve her reader by sharing how she overcame, the lessons she learned, the mistakes she made, what she did right. She gave her readers hope, roused their spirits, and gave suggestions on how overcome their struggle. That is inspirational.

I.S.~Spark!

Think about your story and write any possible lessons, advice, insight, or even a humorous observation. Remember, sometimes humor is the best cure.

Compose

Simply put, nonfiction writing is a narrative prose of provable facts. Whether it is an essay, memoir, biography, or journalistic report, the facts must be true and verifiable. My history textbooks in high school and college were full of facts. It was like chewing tree bark—don't ask. I usually skimmed and highlighted the dates in bold to memorize. Sometimes, reading nonfiction is a chore.

On the other hand, reading creative nonfiction is easy, because this kind of nonfiction prose not only tells the whole truth, but also follows a story arc and uses literary technique. The reason it is better than a report with "just the facts, Ma'am" is because it activates the readers "right brain" and we are drawn into the text.

The left portion of the brain is the analytical, logical, problem solving side. The right portion controls the imagination, emotion, and creativity. Once the right side is engaged and the reader is connected, the left side gets involved in absorbing information and making decisions based on the right side illumination.

Dr. Gary Smalley, one of the country's best-known authors and speakers on family relationships, gave the following example that illustrates just how powerful the right brain influence can be.

In 1940, deer hunting was a twelve-million dollar business. Today that would be over one-hundred-sixty million. However, in 1942 that amount dropped to two million because of one man and one movie. Care to guess what movie? If you guessed, *Bambi*, you're right. In 1940, deer were considered by most people to be a wild animal. In 1942, *Bambi* was a sad and frightened little boy who lost his mommy to a violent death by the big, bad, deer hunter.

It's my opinion that the two million dollars came from *single* men. I get this mental image of all the

"June Cleaver" type wives in frilly aprons standing at the door, arms folded over their chests and their sulky husbands trudging up the stairs, dragging their guns behind them.

Creative nonfiction are true stories written with fiction techniques. The writer has tools that help him delve deep into a story and bring a fuller understanding to the subject, more than a simple reporting of the facts. It is a way to connect with the reader in a cooperative effort to understand those facts.

The creative nonfiction style is criticized by some and applauded by others. The main criticism is that it isn't held to the same journalistic ethics and standards and writers often take artistic license to the point of fabrication. And some have. Ever heard of *A Million Little Pieces* by James Frey? His memoir contained large portions that were wholly untrue and gross exaggeration. *The Smoking Gun,* a website that posts outrageous or obscure information which is oftentimes unreported by the mainstream media, exposed Frey in its article, "A Million Little Lies, Exposing James Frey's Fiction Addiction."

However, on the whole, those who write creative nonfiction are incredible writers and leave the reader wanting more. My favorite writer by far is Rick Bragg. Anything he writes is a great example of this style. He gets personally involved with whatever he is writing and he takes us there. We know what he is thinking, what he is feeling.

Another great example of this style is Frank McCourt's memoir *Angela's Ashes.* He writes about his impoverished childhood in Brooklyn and Limerick City, Ireland. It is a great read, or rent the audio book, read by McCourt to get the full Irish flavor.

As I mentioned earlier, creative nonfiction uses fiction techniques which are:

Setting a scene or an anchor

Description
Emotion
Dialogue
Internalization

One other fiction element is "point-of-view" or POV. This identifies which character is telling the story. The creative nonfiction style offers writers the freedom to express their viewpoints, observations, and opinions.

Let's explore each technique:

Setting a Scene

A scene is where the action happens. It establishes the setting, time, mood, and whose point-of-view we are in. Think about the opening of a movie while the credits are showing. What we see clues us in on where we are, time in history, the mood, and the main character.

Because articles have a limited word count, it is better to use one scene. In the case of inspirational books, where there is the luxury of higher word counts, multiple scenes can be used as long as the they have depth and are complete.

After each scene, which will always involve action, drama, or an emotional reaction, there will follow a sequel. The sequel is the "rest" after the scene where the character regroups, reflects, or processes what happened in the previous scene.

After the sequel a new scene begins. This works in creative nonfiction as well.

Using an Anchor

When writing articles, I use an anchor in my scene, because articles are single-themed and have word count limits. Think snapshot instead of movie. An anchor keeps the story strong, immediate, and understandable, by keeping it in place instead of flying away. Picture yourself holding a helium balloon tied to a string. The balloon can move around, but its range of motion is limited and it can't disappear into the clouds of obscure words. Anchors can be an object, an emotion, an event, a room, a conversation, a person, a quote, anything the story can revolve around.

The Purpose of Scenes and Anchors

They hold the story in place and give focus. It is important to lose all peripheral vision and resist giving information that isn't relevant to what is happening in immediate story. Don't make your reader work to understand what you are saying.

Take my grandpuppy, Kricket, for example. She is a feisty Jack Russell Terrier and has the most expressive chocolate-drop eyes. One never wonders what is on her mind. It is amazing how she communicates that she is "patiently waiting" for that bite of boiled chicken that I am using for a salad to be dropped to the floor.

For an old dog, eleven years and counting, she loves to play. One of her favorite games is to run long figure eights around the yard when I yell, "Run, Kricket, run!" The more I yell the faster she goes.

Let's say you came to visit me and I said, "Oh, you just have to see Kricket's Hershey Kiss eyes! They are simply beautiful."

Your curiosity is roused and you really want to see them. So I whistle for her, but before she gets close enough for you to see, I yell, "Run, Kricket, run!"

Will you be able to see her baby-browns while she scoots across the yard cutting large figure eights? No, of course not. At best, you might catch a glimpse of them when she races by. The only way for you to get a good look at them is for me to pick her up and hold her still.

Too often, when we have something to say in an article we tell our words to run! And the page is filled with unnecessary details and back-story—the history behind the situation we are writing about—making our reader wonder what we are really trying to say.

It is important to hold our story in place with scenes and anchors. They provide our readers a place of reference and make it easy to grasp what we are hoping to convey.

My story, "Wassup?," published in *Chicken Soup for the Mother and Son Soul*, is a good example of a conversation being the anchor with just enough flexibility to make a point without losing focus. Let's take a look at it.

WASSUP?

One of the challenges I encountered with my son during his teen years was meaningful communication. At the age of sixteen, he no longer spoke in traditional sentences. Rather, he spoke in one or two words that conveyed the main idea. For instance, upon meeting a friend in the mall, an exchange would go something like this:

"Wassup?"
"Chillin'."
"Cool."
"Later."
"Later, man."

After finally comprehending this new means of "teen-speak," it became clear to me why he always got this glazed look when I tried to talk to him. Too many words, I suppose, for his hormone-soaked adolescent mind to process. So instead of fighting it, I decided to try it. One morning I walked into his room, pointed in the general vicinity of the floor, which hadn't seen daylight in weeks, and said, "Room, rank, clean, today."

Worked like a charm!

Even though I'd cracked the code, I still longed to connect with him in the traditional, full-sentence way, but how? The answer came quite by accident. Late one night, I decided to pop some corn and watch a chick-flick. The buttery aroma drifted into his room and enticed him to investigate the source.

Without warning, he plopped beside me on the couch and put his huge paw in my bowl. The mantle clock chimed midnight. Something about the bell tolling twelve and the warm, fluffy kernels really loosened his lips. The kid talked about everything. He told me things I wanted to know and some things I'd rather not have known.

He said his girl dumped him. I didn't know he had one. Oh well, she didn't deserve him anyway.

He talked about his career choice—a video game tester. Hmm, maybe this wouldn't be a good time to talk about medical school.

Last week, his best friend threw a cool party while his parents were gone. No parents? Mental note to self—never leave town.

Conversation flowed for at least two hours. I was exhilarated. In heaven. On cloud nine. Finally, we were communication in full sentences. We connected. I crossed the barrier with popcorn at midnight.

The next morning my heart still sang of the progress made just a few short hours earlier. I couldn't contain my excitement when I called him to breakfast. What would we discuss? The possibilities were endless.

However, I realized moments like the night before were small gifts to tide me over until my son achieved manhood, when he walked in the kitchen and said, "Wassup?"

Did you recognize the anchor of my story? It was the problem of meaningful, full-sentence conversation. In the introduction, I wrote a brief account about bumping into his friend and their conversation and about our "meeting of the minds" concerning his room. Each account was succinctly written. There was no need for me to describe my son's friend, the stores in the mall, our conversation before the friend met us or afterward. You got the idea that his room was a disaster without me describing the blobs of toothpaste that had turned into pottery on his bathroom counter or the science project growing in the bottom of his favorite mug. By simply writing how the floor hadn't seen daylight in weeks got the point across.

A snapshot, not a movie.

> **I.S.~Spark!**
> Choose an anchor for your story and write it in your journal.

Description

Many make the mistake of using a chain of adjectives when trying to describe something. But there is a better way. Inside the attic of our minds are five keys that will open our reader's memories and make our job much easier. These keys are the senses. And if we use these keys effectively, even if we only use one, the reader will add all the others by remembering their own experience.

When listening to someone at a conference teach fiction writing, we often hear them say, "Show! Don't tell!" Why? Because it is easy to overuse adjectives to describe something and it's just as easy for our reader to zone out when reading those familiar descriptions.

How do we show? We use the senses. By doing this our readers pull from their own experiences and "fill in the blanks," so to speak, mentally embellishing what we write. A movie plays in their head showing images of days gone by, tastes, aromas, sensations, and sounds. They laugh, they cry, they may sigh, but most importantly, they connect with us.

Connect—there's that word again. But this is one of the most important aspects of inspirational writing. In the "Wassup?" story, could you smell the popcorn or see flickering lights from the television screen in the dark room? Maybe you heard the clock chime midnight. You were there with me.

In my "Power of a Drop of Ink Writing Workshop," I conduct a little experiment with the attendees to drive this point home. I read a scene about a young man in his mother's kitchen. It includes the five senses. Then I ask volunteers what they saw, heard, smelled, tasted, and felt. I never cease to be amazed by the wide variety of answers. Why not give it a try?

> **Spark!**
>
> Read the following scenes:

I followed my nose to the kitchen and found Mom bent over the oven.

"Morning, Mom."

She straightened and turned. "Rob, you're up early. How about some coffee? Fresh ground. Just made."

My gaze went to the hot loaf of cinnamon bread she held within mitted hands. "Sounds good." I kept my eye on the pan.

A pleased smile brightened her face. Feeding people, especially me, was her purpose in life. "All right, I get the hint. But get yourself some coffee."

With a quick flip, she turned the loaf onto the platter, took a knife and cut two large slices. Spicy steam escaped and mingled with the aroma of the Kona Blend I poured in my cup.

After slathering the slices with sweet cream butter she handed me a piece. Butter escaped the corners of my mouth when I bit into the tender bread.

Man, it just didn't get any better than this.

What movie played in your head?

Describe the kitchen:

Describe Momma:

Describe Rob:

What you heard:

What you smelled:

What you touched:

What it felt like:

Look at your responses. How much of what you wrote was actually in the paragraph? I'll wager not much. At least, that is what I have found in my workshops. One gentleman said he saw a woodstove and the faint hint of smoke combined with the cinnamon and coffee. Another heard a radio playing. A lady saw a windowed "nook" with a small table covered with a red checkered tablecloth.

The amazing thing is how differently everyone saw that scene. They saw it from their memory, and that connected them with the paragraph. I wrote a few lines and they mentally wrote a page.

If I had written this with "just the facts" it would have read like this:

I walked into the kitchen for breakfast. Mom had baked cinnamon bread and made coffee. She cut me a slice and I put butter on it before taking a bite. It just didn't get better than this.

Kind of flat and boring, if you ask me. Worse yet, easy to skim over.

> **Spark!**
> Practice using the senses:

Free write a list of sensations and memories for each one of the following words.

Snow

Lemons

Puppies

Train whistle

Autumn

Ocean

Flies

Butterfinger candy bar

Doorbell

From the free writing above choose the senses and/or memory for the words below. If you leave some blank, that is fine.

Snow:
See
Hear
Taste
Touch
Smell

Lemons:
See
Hear
Taste
Touch
Smell

Puppies:
See
Hear
Taste
Touch
Smell

Train whistle:
See
Hear
Taste
Touch
Smell

Autumn:
See
Hear
Taste
Touch
Smell

Ocean:
See
Hear
Taste
Touch
Smell

Flies:
See
Hear
Taste
Touch
Smell

Butterfinger Candy Bar:
See
Hear
Taste
Touch
Smell

Door Bell:
See
Hear
Taste
Touch
Smell

For extra practice, try and think of descriptions or memories to fill in beside the senses you left blank. This will be an excellent resource for you to return to when writing.

Reclaim Wonder

There are times we are stumped when we try to come up with something fresh in our descriptions. We keep using the same wore out phrases. A remedy for that is to tap into the curiosity we had as children.

I remember watching a little boy walk to his house each day after getting off the school bus. He walked with is head thrown back looking at the trees, the clouds, birds. Often, he'd just stop and stare. I wondered what he saw.

One day, I decided to find out. I walked outside, laid under a tree and observed. The first thing I noticed was all the different shades of green, even though in reality all the leaves were the same color. The sunlight cast the illusion of spring, emerald, and forest greens. Some even seemed transparent. The wind made them dance and whisper. I wondered what secrets a leaf would have to tell.

Birds flew in and out building nests in the protection of the canopy. I sat up, not wanting their by-product in my face, if you know what I mean. They hopped from branch to branch, chattering until finally deciding on the perfect one for their new home. What were they looking for? What made the perfect branch? And how does instinct work?

It is fascinating to think that their chromosomes are coded with the engineering capability to weave a nest that will withstand the most powerful storm. I wish I'd had that kind of instinct in all of my college classes. Studying was such a damper on my creativity.

That afternoon, I reclaimed my "inner child," heightening my curiosity and observation powers.

Spark!

Reclaim the wonder of a child:

Watch children in the age range of 2-5 play outside. Write about their wonder:

What do they seem to find interesting?

Describe how they watch.

Look at things the way they do. Be a blank slate. No opinions, no educated foreknowledge, just wonder.

Write what you see, your feelings, thoughts, and imaginations.

Pick a flower. What does it make you think of?

What does its fragrance remind you of? It could be a place, a person, a moment.

Feel the petals, take the flower apart and write about it.

Describe the flower they way you would to a person born blind.

Have you ever watched an infant who just discovered her hands? The expression of wonder on her face is intoxicating. We see our hands every day and hardly give them a thought unless they hurt or need some kind of cosmetic attention.

Study your hands. Spread your fingers and look at the back, then turn it palm up.

How would you describe it to an alien from Mars?

Flex your fingers. Turn your hand over and flex again. Freely move your fingers at random and watch. Make them look like they are blowing in the wind. Wave them like they are on the ocean. Do the hula with your hands. Now write about the toy on the end of your arm.

Write any memories your hands or someone else's brings to you.

List all the synonyms for hand (like farmhand for example) that you can think of and why you think they apply.

> **Spark!**
> Sharpen your observation skills:

How many times do we look, but not see? Life bubbles around us in a rich brew of laughter, tears, excitement, and awe. Have we drunk from its elixir? Life is woven with stories, cultures, history and art. Are we warmed by its fabric? Do we notice it at all? If not, it's time.

Grab a notebook and pen, then go to a Barnes and Noble coffee shop, my favorite spot. However, I suppose any coffee shop would do. Buy a latte or whatever you like, and sit where you can observe and hear the people around you. Choose a person or a table of friends and look like an innocent beverage sipper instead of an eavesdropper. Answer the following questions:

How are they alike?

How are they different?

Name the mood of each individual.

How can you tell?

What are they talking about? (if you can hear, of course)

Describe their facial expressions.

Describe their hand gestures.

Now choose someone else or another table and do the same.

Observe the barista—a coffee bartender. What kind of mood is he/she in? How can you tell?

While savoring your latte, wrap your mind around this:

The population of the world is estimated at seven billion people.

We are alike in that the majority of us are born with two eyes, a nose, a mouth, two ears, two arms, two hands, ten fingers, two legs, two feet, ten toes, etc.

But every one of the seven billion people has different fingerprints.

Because of the complex structure of the capillaries in the retina no one has the same retinal pattern. Even identical twins do not share a similar pattern!

Seven billion people, the same and different. Amazing!

Write your thoughts about this incredible fact.

Take a blanket and spread it out under a large, spreading tree. Answer the following questions:

How many shades of green do you see?

What do you hear?

What do you smell?

What kind of wildlife makes their home in that tree?

Now daydream. If this tree could speak, what memories would it have of the things that happened under its branches?

Emotion

We experience many emotions during our waking hours and even in our dreams. Why not include them in our article? Keep in mind—if our writing doesn't move us in some way emotionally, it will not move or inspire our reader.

Writing emotions is more than telling our affective state of consciousness such as: *I am happy, I was sad, she made me angry, the storm frightened me to death.* We don't want to give our reader a reason to skim over familiar words like happy, sad, angry, or frightened. We want to stimulate their memories so they will connect with us.

Remember the admonishment, *"Show! Don't tell!"* We do this by describing the physical effect, body language, or gestures that accompany a particular emotion. Think about how we often have a physiological response to emotions. Goosebumps raise the hair on our arms when we are afraid, or our face flushes and turns red when we are angry.

Body language is how we communicate what is inside without saying a word. Anger makes us clench our jaw. When we are excited, our breath comes in gasps as we fling our arms and jump up and down.

By describing physical responses and body language, we are creating an image that will connect with our readers.

Instead of writing: **"I was so worried."**

Write: **"I paced the floor and wrung my hands till they ached."**

See how the second example makes it easier to connect? Does pacing the floor and wringing hands bring back any recollections? If you've ever raised teenagers I'm sure it does. More than once I sat on the front porch in the wee hours of the morning, rocking and waiting for my curfew breaking offenders. My body tense, nausea waved over me while my mind filled with images of them bleeding on the side of the road. Even as I worried, anger seethed inside me and I wanted to slap them silly as soon as I saw they were home safe and sound. I have to admit, relief at the sight of them overruled the "slap them silly notion."

With each emotion we experience varied physical responses in our bodies and use our bodies to express those emotions through facial expression, gestures, and positioning. It is easy to identify the emotions that are surging through perfect strangers by watching their body language and gestures.

This is how to "show" emotions instead of telling. Describe the physical response inside our bodies, our gestures, and what we see others doing.

Following are several emotions for us to examine and hopefully "jump start" your ideas. A space is provided after each emotion to write your own thoughts about them.

Happy

When I'm happy, my body is relaxed and a sense of well-being fills me. I may even feel a sudden surge of energy. Colors are vibrant, food tastes better, my mind is at peace, my soul is light and my attitude is positive. I'm patient and generous toward others and sensitive to their needs.

I can tell when others are happy because they smile; causing little lines crinkle under their eyes and their cheeks to plump. Their step is livelier and they may speak faster and their voice is more animated. They may clap their hands and jump up and down.

Happy people laugh and joke. We southerners cannot resist touching your arm while talking. Heck, we will probably hug you.

Your thoughts:

Love/affection

In the English language the word "love" can be used for a multitude of meanings. I can say that I love God, I love my family, I love crepe myrtle trees, I love coffee, and I love cream-filled chocolate covered doughnuts (yum) and each statement sends a very different message. Keep this in mind when writing about love.

My love for God is rooted in my devotion, gratitude, and honor for Him. No matter how I feel day-to-day my relationship with God never changes except that as I grow older He grows dearer to me. The same is true for my family. I love my family with my life and all that is in my power. They may hurt my feelings or let me down at times, as I do them, but my love for them is constant.

I love crepe myrtle trees, coffee, and sinful pastries because they make me *feel* good. I wrote all of this to emphasize the importance of assigning the right response to the right form of love.

My love for God and my family would be action words. God's love wraps me in peace. It burns through my darkness and reveals truth, exposing the lies that blind me. Family love is intense and often frustrating. It is being one unit, but forging our own paths. It is a force that sharpens us but during the sharpening process sparks fly.

My love for my husband is life itself. It is like the ocean, deep, with occasional crashing waves, comfortable as an old sweatshirt, surprising like the sudden heat when biting down on a hot peppercorn while eating a salad.

My love for my children is a tender lullaby, but should someone harm them in any way it raises on its haunches fierce as a mother grizzly.

Nature, good food, music, art, books, are the swinging hammocks under the coolness of shady trees on hot summer days, the cold condensation on the sides of my iced tea glass.

My expression of love is compassion, concern. I make eye contact with others. They convey the message "I see you," they may sparkle, they may fill with tears. My mouth might turn up at the corners or it might stay shut. My body language is open, leaning forward, with hands that span the gap between us. It must never be in a posture of judgment.

Your thoughts:

Lust

Lust wears many masks. For some it is a passionate, enthusiastic zeal. Others burn with unquenchable lewdness and sexual desire. Then there are those with excessive craving for power. Like love, we have to be sure which mask we are describing.

Those with the lust for life live life with abandon. They dance about like a leaf in the wind, faces to the sky, arms held wide as if to embrace the earth. They are flamboyant, daring, and draw others like moths to a flame.

Lust is more readily recognized by the greedy, self-serving, emotion. A blazing fire demanding others feed it, and when they do it burns them. It smolders with covetousness, want, desire, and manipulation to have its way.

The face of lust leers, eyes narrow, and the mouth twists in a sneer. Lust reaches out to lure prey hiding, the claws that will destroy its victim.

Love is all about others. Lust is all about self.

Your thoughts:

Sadness/ Depression

Sadness is like a heavy cloak, damp and dark. I am tired and want to escape in sleep. Tears rise unbidden to the surface, my throat tightens and aches. Breathing is tedious. The oxygen seems to have left the room. Food is tasteless, yet I eat mindlessly. Some lose their appetite all together. Not me. I'm oblivious to the things around me. My focus is on me and I get irritable. Past disappointments and offenses oppress my mind. Hope is gone. Just let me hide.

Sad people gaze down. Their mouths droop at the corners and there is no lift to their brows. They walk like weights are on their ankles, their shoulders slump, and they speak in monotone.

Depression is all the above, but deeper. It sends us into an emotional prison where there are no windows, no air, no light, only darkness. The only sound is the voice of self-destruction and we listen.

Your thoughts:

Shame

Shame is a violation of cultural and/or social values. It is the painful feeling that comes from our consciousness that we or someone else has done something dishonorable, improper, or absurd. Our bodies are slack. We turn away, lower our head, and fix our gaze on the ground. The heat from our blush creeps up our neck and covers our face.

Embarrassment is similar to shame, but is usually caused by something happening in public, whereas shame can be precipitated by an act known only to oneself.

Your thoughts:

Anger

This is probably the easiest to express, because there are so many physical changes. Anger and fear produce adrenalin needed for survival's "flight or fight" response. Our breathing increases and provides oxygen to the brain, blood is detoured away from internal organs and sent to our muscles for strength, our pupils dilate to sharpen our vision. Rational thought disengages and our thinking becomes disoriented.

When I'm angry my breathing is rapid and shallow making me feel a little dizzy, my heart pounds, the veins in my temples throb, and my pulse races. Muscles tense and my chest gets tight. Sometimes I shake, clench my jaw and squeeze my hands into fists.

Angry people are easy to spot. They glare from under lowered eyebrows pulled together forming wrinkles in the forehead. Their faces are flushed, even sweating. You can see the tension. Their lips are pressed together and their chins jut out. People often try to disguise their annoyance but it is easy to spot because of their intense eye-contact and folded arms across their chest.

Even from a distance you can recognize when someone is angry. Their thunderous voice roars while they gesture with erratic arm sweeps, shaking fists, pounding tables or walls, throwing things. Irate individuals will invade their victims' personal space by leaning in, and may even poke them in the chest.

Whew! I'm exhausted.

Your thoughts:

Frustration

This is anger's second cousin and can escalate to anger. It builds like a fire in middle earth and only we are aware of it. Mild irritations scrub our soul, but we can ignore it for a while. It's that one last rub that gives vent to our volcano and it blows, spewing expletives in the air like ash and molten lava sarcasms—and then it's over. Frustration may point the finger and blame others, or it might quit and give up—depending on that person's temperament.

Frustrated people are distracted, edgy, and have short fuses. They run their hands through their hair, rub their faces, and slam their hands on their hips or whatever is close by. Some people kick something like a table leg or a wall. Really bad people kick cats. Shame on them.

Your thoughts:

Fear

We have a love/hate relationship with fear—liking the emotional thrill of a scary story or movie, while hating the reality of terror threats or walking down an abandoned street on a starless night. Just as with anger, adrenaline is pumped into our bodies. The same physical responses occur, but fear dilates our lungs to allow more air flow and we go on autopilot and flee, even though our brains haven't consciously figured out why or from what. For some reason, goose bumps rise on our skin. Each little hair has a tiny muscle that contracts. That is what animals do to keep warm or look larger and fiercer. I'm not sure what purpose that serves in a human, but it works for a cat. Also, our mouths go dry.

In a non-threatening situation, fear can be an astute and focused reaction, or it can creep over us like a dark, menacing fog that we can't quite pin-point. Both create inertia, immobilizing us, clouding our minds and make us irrational. I hear my heartbeat in my ears and instead of breathing fast, I barely breathe at all.

Fear is most noticeably expressed in our eyes. We lift our eyebrows and our eyes widen until the white almost circles the iris. We usually put out our hands, as if to fend off danger, or we may put them on our face or press them against our chest. I usually lean back.

Nervousness is a result of fear, as is dread. Show nerves by writing about sweaty palms, fidgeting, bouncing our knee up and down while sitting, fluttering stomach, etc.

Your thoughts:

Surprise

This is an unexpected burst of emotion that can be rooted in fear or happiness. If someone jumps out at me with a knife I will react in fear. If people jump from behind a chair with party hats on and yell, "surprise," I will jump physically and a little happy thrill will tingle through me. I might feel disoriented, a little euphoric, even confused but as it sinks in I'll experience all the traits of happiness.

Surprise's expression has the same wide-eyed look and gasping through a gaping mouth. The most common gesture is to clasp our hands to our chests or our face. We might even flail our arms in the air like when our basketball team is behind by one point and our guy makes a basket just as the final buzzer rings.

Your thoughts:

Worry

Most parents are well acquainted with this emotion. A close relative to fear, worry is that fog of "what if's." I read someone's comment that worry is like negative meditation because we take the situation we are worried about and mentally play every facet of possible outcomes. Anxious thoughts collide and tangle in our minds making it hard to discern the truth. Mental voices screaming "doom" makes peace impossible.

When I worry my stomach gets queasy, my heart palpitates, and my breathing is shallow. My mind races and I pace, unable to focus. I cry easy, get angry even easier.

I clasp my hands and hold them close to my stomach. Sometimes I wring them. I stare at nothing while the obsessive videos play in my mind.

Worry's expression is mostly in the upper part of the face. Eyebrows are drawn together creasing the skin between them into "worry lines." The eyes may be slightly hooded, staring but not seeing. The mouth is neutral, perhaps slightly open or pouting. A worried person usually puts there hand to their mouth or forehead.

Your thoughts:

Hate

This emotion destroys its host. It is like cancer eating away at the soul. Some feel they have a right to hate for something that was done to them by another. What they do not realize is that the hate is killing them more than it is hurting the offender. Hate can rage, but more often it is subtle, hiding in the dark corners of our mind, patiently waiting for when we are most vulnerable. It speaks quiet, convincing lies, and if we listen it poisons our minds and overtakes us.

Hate grows from a wound, it burns and scars. We can be having a perfect day until the object of our hate comes into view and the burning, the churning, the pain begins. Dark shadows descend and our hate deepens. It replaces rational thought with destructive feelings.

Our very appearance changes with hate. Our expression is hard, detached. Body language is closed. But the fire burns inside and may explode at the slightest provocation.

Your thoughts:

Jealousy

This emotion is often confused with envy, and while they are similar they are rooted in two different scenarios. Jealousy is about something we already have, envy is about what someone else has and we want it. An emotion that fuels jealousy is fear—of losing someone or something—so all the attributes of fear will apply. Passion and anger may also apply.

It is the self-talk that gives birth to jealousy, what we tell ourselves about what might happen until we believe it has happened. The expression of jealousy is to appear as if we are not looking, but in reality we are watching from the corner of our eyes. We huff, sigh, shake our head, pace. Our insides churn, our hearts palpitate, as we deal with all the negative thoughts bombarding our brains. Our chests and throats tighten and we have to swallow.

The best way to show jealousy when writing is including the "self-talk" what is referred to as "internalization" later on in this section.

Your thoughts:

Spark!

Below are sentences that "tell" emotion. Rewrite them and "show" emotion. It may take more than one sentence to do this. Use the information I gave and your notes.

Happy

Scarlett O'Hara was happy that Ashley would be attending the barbeque.

Love/Affection

She loved Ashley and wanted to run to him and stop him before he reached Melanie.

Sad/Depressed

When Scarlett heard Ashley was engaged to his cousin, Melanie, she was sad.

Anger

Scarlett threw a vase across the room in anger.

Frustration

In frustration she wondered how he could love that mousey little thing instead of her?

Fear

Fear welled up inside her when a stranger sat up on the couch.

Surprise

Surprised by his presence she demanded to know his name.

Worry

Scarlett worried that Rhett would tell her secret.

Lust

Rhett looked at Scarlett with lust.

Jealousy

After Rhett and Scarlett married he was jealous of her.

Hate

He hated Ashley Wilkes.

Shame

Ashley felt shame when he kissed Scarlett.

> **Spark!**
>
> Go back to the **Spark! Sharpen your observation skills** on page 53. Reread what you wrote and identify the emotions that were present.

Dialogue

Without fail, when I speak to groups about adding dialogue to their nonfiction there is at least one person who has a problem with this suggestion. Their concern is not being able to recall word for word what was said, or if anything was said at all. After all, nonfiction is supposed to nothing but the truth, right?

Yes. However, even if we are writing about something that happened the day before, we probably won't write what was said word-for-word. I have a big family and during the holidays our home is buzzing with conversations. Suppose if, at the end of the day, I took each person aside and asked what was said at the dinner table. Without a doubt they would tell me essentially the same thing but in a different way, using different words.

It is rare in a social situation that some conversation doesn't happen. Therefore, it is appropriate to add dialogue that fits the situation as long as it doesn't change the facts and distort the truth. For instance, if you write about a reunion you attended many years ago, include conversation normally heard at reunions, such as: "Is this your boy? My how he's grown. How many children do you have? You haven't aged a bit. What are you doing now?" Do you see how any of these statements can be included without changing any facts? We may not be able to tell verbatim what happened yesterday, so are we to never talk about it? I hope not!

Use dialogue. It makes your piece genuine and provides a friendly, conversational appeal. This is also a great way to include more extensive information, emotions, and descriptions that are needed for clarity, but if used outside of dialogue would be tedious and telling.

As I mentioned earlier, my story, *Connected by Love*, was published in *Chicken Soup for the Father and Daughter Soul*. The anchor is the relationship I have with my stepfather. I can't swear this was the exact word for word dialogue I had with him that day, but it is the basis of our conversation.

If I had written this story with just the facts it would have looked like this:

CONNECTED BY LOVE

I had a party for our new granddaughter and a friend noticed that she looked like my husband and dad, but actually we are not genetically related. Then, after the party, Dad and I went to the porch, drank coffee, listened to the night sounds, watched fireflies dance, and talked. In the course of our conversation, I remembered that the same mistake was made when I was a little girl. Even my grandmother forgot that Dad was not a blood-relative. I brought that up to Dad and he remembered too.

But it wasn't until I got up to refill our cups that it hit me, when fate dealt the same blow to me as it did my mother years ago and I was left a single parent, there waiting in the wings was Neal—a man who would love my daughter as fully as my dad loved me. The power of love knitted three generations together so much so that we even looked alike.

Although life didn't connect us genetically, love did.

Notice how much better it is with dialogue:

CONNECTED BY LOVE

"Dad, it just doesn't get any better than this, does it?" I leaned over his shoulder as he rocked my three-month-old granddaughter, his great-granddaughter, Elizabeth.

"No, Sis, it sure doesn't."

It was the day of her dedication, and my house was filled with family and friends, all coming to meet our newest family member. As we admired her, my husband, Neal, and our daughter, Amanda, walked over with a family friend.

"Okay, Charles," said Neal with a grin, "my turn." Dad handed her to him so our friend could get a better look. The friend stroked her cheek with his finger and said, "She sure looks like you, Neal. She has your eyes." Then he nodded at my dad. "Great-grandpa, you can't deny her either. She has your mouth and chin."

We smiled and gave each other a knowing look—neither man was a blood relative to my daughter and me. Mom married Dad with I was three. I married

Neal when Amanda was two. And yet, I had to agree with our friend that Elizabeth did look like them both.

That evening Mom and Neal stayed in the kitchen to finish straightening up, but Dad and I opted for coffee on the porch. We sat in the rockers and enjoyed the twilight as the soft breeze caressed our faces. After a while, Dad broke the silence.

"You know, Sis, today reminded me of when our family would gather at the farm."

I nodded. "Yes, it does."

A cicada began his raspy call, taking me back to my dad's old home place, where we would visit his mother and father, known to me as Granny and Granddaddy. While rocking, lost in memories of days there as a child, I remembered a conversation Mom had with Granny in the kitchen back then. I sipped my coffee and rocked. "Dad, isn't it funny how people have always thought I looked like you?"

"What's that, Hon?"

"I remember Mom remarking to Granny how surprised she was that I was so tall since she was only five feet tall. Granny, never looking up from her biscuit bowl, said, 'Why, she got her height from Charles.'"

Dad chuckled. "She never thought of you as anything but my biological child. As a matter of fact, I haven't either."

Tears welled in my eyes.

Then Dad asked, "Do you remember at Granny's funeral when I introduced you, Neal, and Amanda to my cousin and she said Amanda was the image of me and Neal?"

"I'd forgotten that." I patted his knee. "Well, Dad, I guess you and Neal have such strong genes that they leap genetic barriers with a single bound."

By now fireflies lit the night while crickets and tree frogs sang in full chorus.

"More coffee?" I asked.

"Sounds good."

I took the cups and went inside to refill them. When I started back outside, I saw Dad through the window. Tears freely ran down my cheeks. I watched him as he rocked and thought about how lucky I was to have such a man for my father.

Then it hit me. When fate dealt the same blow to me as it did my mother years ago and I was left a single parent, there, waiting in the wings was Neal—a man who would love my daughter as fully as my dad loved me. The power of love knitted three generations together so much so that we even looked alike.

Although life didn't connect us genetically, love did.

I.S.~Spark!

Write the dialogue you remember during the time of your story.

Write possible dialogue appropriate to the setting without changing the facts.

Internalization

I read where an average of sixty thousand thoughts floods our minds each day. Hmmm, how do they measure that? And who are they? Oops, I wrote my thoughts.

Did you connect with them? Be honest, I'll bet you thought the same thing.

Our self-talk—internalization—is an effective way to express our emotions and observations. It gives a personal, even confidential, feel between the writer and the reader. It is also a great way to express emotion without it feeling "sappy" or gratuitous. If you like to write humor, this is a very effective tool. It adds punch to the funny lines.

I used this method in my humor article, Hormone Hell. All the internalization is in italics.

HORMONE HELL

Hormones are evil. They lie in ambush, waiting to attack even the most saintly of women, without warning.

My first assault happened while speaking at a ladies luncheon. The room grew warm—a little too warm. A fine mist broke out on my face and pooled into drops of sweat. Fire erupted under my skin and spread from my dripping head to my sweaty feet. Black mascara tracks rolled down my cheeks. Like the Wicked Witch of the West, I melted in front of forty women.

Great. I've been ambushed by hormone demons. Wasn't this supposed to happen in my fifties? A pool, I gotta find a pool.

I finished my presentation, excused myself, and frantically searched for a room to remove every article of clothing acceptable in polite society. Off came my jacket, slip, bra, shoes and pantyhose. I looked like Superman in a phone booth.

That night after supper I sprawled under the oscillating fan—sweating. My husband, on the other hand, relaxed in the recliner oblivious to my pain.

He makes me sick. Mother Nature isn't fair. She loves her sons the best. He's all cool and comfy while I endure hormonal damnation with menopausal devils tap dancing on every nerve.

I got up, stalked to the kitchen and stuck my head in the freezer.

It isn't fair. I endured cramps, PMS, and gave birth five times—by C-section no less

Mother Nature must have disapproved of my little outburst. As punishment she sent me night sweats.

For those of you who aren't familiar with this phenomenon, night sweats are fiery nocturnal combustions that explode every few hours all night long. My bedtime routine drastically changed. I dropped the thermostat to thirty degrees, set a jug of ice water on the nightstand, and turned the ceiling fan on high. The only part of my routine that remained the same was our goodnight kiss, even though his lips were blue.

Every couple of hours my internal sauna kicked in. I threw off the comforter, held my damp face to the fan, and gulped water which, of course, necessitated a trip to the bathroom. After another glass of cold water, I crawled into bed where my husband lay in fetal position, shaking violently.

"I-is i-it safe to p-pull up the c-c-comforter now?" he asked.

"Sure Hon."

Hmmm, there is something strangely satisfying seeing him this way.

Thankfully, I'm adjusting to menopause. However, my husband isn't. I've noticed a change in him. He seems sluggish—irritable.

During breakfast this morning I looked into his bloodshot eyes.

"Sleep well, my love?"

He scowled. "How long does this menopause thing last? I've got to get some rest."

I smiled before sipping my iced coffee.

Take that Mother Nature.

"Could be years. Sorry, Baby."

The table groaned as he pushed himself up to leave. I won't report what he muttered. I know it's wrong of me, but I just can't feel sorry for him. Quite the opposite, really. I feel vindicated. After all, if we women must suffer hormone hell, at least men should have hell to pay.

Remember, internalization (self-talk) is a great place to show emotion. For instance, "It just doesn't get better than this" shows happiness and contentment. "Where's a rock, I need to crawl under it" shows embarrassment.

> **Spark!**
> In your own words write a thought that expresses each emotion without using its name.

Happy:

Sad/Depressed:

Anger:

Frustration:

Fear:

Surprise:

Worry:

Love/Affection:

Lust:

Jealousy:

Hate:

Shame:

> **I.S.~Spark!**
> Think about your story and jot down ideas for internalization.

Our Gift

In the beginning of the book I asked you to write three goals for your story. Now it is time to give your readers that gift. Your gift may be in the form of a simple lesson that gives subtle instruction or conveys some kind of insight. It may be an epiphany, a word of encouragement and hope. And, as I wrote earlier, you may give the medicine of a merry heart with humor—something that brightens your reader's day.

The important thing to remember is to never be preachy or your message glaring. My story, *Down And Out*, was published in *Chicken Soup for the Mothers of Preschooler's Soul*. I saw the story call-out on their site I knew immediately what I wanted to write about. It was an experience that changed the way I lived my life and I wanted to encourage other mothers to make the same change. My message is subtle, but I think you will recognize it. Let's see if you do:

DOWN AND OUT

Thursday started like any other day of the school week, with one exception. It was also "Mother's Day Out" which meant that instead dressing two of my children, I had to dress all five. Two went to grade school, and my three preschoolers went to the church where blessed babysitters ministered to harried mothers like me, who needed a day of errand-running, free of strollers, whining, and endless trips to the potty.

After waving goodbye to my two oldest on the school bus, I turned my attention to the other three. It took an hour to change diapers, wash faces, comb hair, and dress them. Finally they were ready, and I secured the baby in his carrier.

"Ok, let's go," I called. Walking past the kitchen, I spotted my three-year-old on the table with both arms in the economy-size grape jelly up to the elbows. Groaning, I set the baby down, snatched my son off the table, held him over the sink and sprayed him off.

Finally getting my little group together, I picked up the carrier and herded the other two down the hall towards the car. As I passed in front of the large mirror hanging over the couch I caught my reflection. Who was that woman? Dressed in a baggy sweat suit, hair pulled back in a haphazard ponytail, no lipstick, no earrings. Before becoming the mother of preschoolers, I wouldn't have even thought of going out in public looking like that. Oh, well, no time to worry about it. I wiped grape jelly off my cheek.

On the way to the church, I looked over my shoulder to check on the children and the sour smell of spit-up assaulted my nose. Before preschoolers, I wore the fragrance, "White Shoulders," Now I smelled like parmesan cheese.

In the parking lot I got the kids out of the car. With the baby carrier hanging on my left arm, my five-year-old holding on to my sweatshirt, I took my three-year-old with my free hand and we trudged up the church stairs. Quite a workout. Before preschoolers, I worked out in a gym.

The children ran to their respective rooms. I glanced at my watch—9:00 a.m. I had till 3:00 p.m. to get all on my list accomplished. Mother's Day Out seemed more like Mother's Minute Out.

As I turned to leave, I noticed a colorful gift bag on a table by the door with my name attached. Inside was a darling mug. It was white with tiny yellow rose buds scattered around the middle. Printed on the inside rim was a little duck. I couldn't help but smile.

Who could this be from?

The note read: To a wonderful mother who deserves some time to herself. Go home; enjoy a cup of tea with your favorite magazine. Today is your day.

Without warning, tears welled and slid down my cheeks. Someone understood. Even though being a mother was what I always wanted to be, it was still hard, often thankless, work. This anonymous person reminded me that, although I wore many hats—wife, mother, daughter, friend—I was still the same person underneath who needed to be cared for as well.

I looked at my list—nothing there that couldn't wait. Orange spice tea and a Southern Living Magazine on the front porch became the priority. From now on Thursday would be Mother's Day Off.

If you guessed the lesson was that young mothers should take care of themselves you guessed right. However, there is another lesson here. Be sensitive to others like the anonymous angel was to me!

Spark!

Review "Down and Out" and identify:

Internalization

Emotions

Any other lesson or encouragement?

Practice, Practice, Practice

Now let's put everything covered in this book into practice by using my favorite *Chicken Soup* story that was published in *Chicken Soup for the Soul, Recipes for Busy Moms,* by identifying:

> The anchor
> Description
> Emotion
> Dialogue
> Internalization
> My Gift to the Readers (there is more than one)

You may want to use different highlighters for each element, or write the answers on a separate sheet of paper.

MY CULINARY EPIPHANY

There are many important "firsts" in life—first step, first word, first kiss, and first turkey—the Thanksgiving kind.

My husband, Neal, and I always went over to my parents for Thanksgiving. We brought the green bean casserole and the kids, Mom did everything else. But the holiday cooking mantel was passed along to me when we were transferred to another city. That didn't bother me, after all, how hard could it be?

Memories of waking to the savory aroma of roasting turkey and the sounds of marching bands on television filled my mind. Mom's face had a rosy glow while preparing for Thanksgiving, from enthusiasm, I supposed. She didn't seem to mind cooking such an extensive meal. Why should I? Plus, she wrote clear, step-by-step instructions for me to follow. A cinch.

Thanksgiving week finally arrived and I pulled out my instructions. First, I had to find the "perfect turkey". One that would feed us and our five children, plus provide ample leftovers for sandwiches, soup, tetrazzini, and any other fascinating dish I could dream up. I bought a twenty-eight pounder.

Next on the "to do" list—thaw him.

Naively, I thought that would only take a few hours on the counter, till my food safety scientist husband nixed that plan as a major violation and told me it would take a week to defrost a bird that big in the refrigerator.

I panicked. Thanksgiving was in two days. I needed a quick defrost method. Neal suggested his granny's technique of putting the turkey in the tub and filling it with cold water. Sounded good to me. I had plenty to do in the meantime.

Later that afternoon, we heard strange noises came from the bathroom.

Thud, splash, thud.

Neal and I ran to the bathroom and found a diaper floating on the flooded floor. Alarmed, I shoved back the shower curtain to find our two-year-old son laying on top of the turkey pushing himself from one end of the tub to the other, like a bucking bird rodeo. All of his cheeks were pink and shiny.

I grabbed our son off the main course. A strange foreboding followed me.

The rest of the day and into the night, I chopped, diced, sliced, mixed, rolled, sautéed, simmered, boiled and baked. I realized something—Mom's rosy glow wasn't because of the enthusiasm. It was heat exhaustion. I collapsed into bed at midnight.

The alarm was unusually loud at five a.m. Thanksgiving morning. I crawled out of bed and felt my way down the hall to the bathroom to get the turkey out of the tub. In my sleep deprived stupor, I hoisted him on my hip. Glacier water spilled down my nylon gown making it cling like a second skin, setting every nerve in my body on red alert. I won't repeat the words I silently screamed.

After peeling off the wrappers, I stared, shocked by the sight in front of me. I'd never seen a naked turkey before. The only ones I'd ever seen wore a nice, crispy, brown skin. This cold, clammy, thing was pale and pimply. Everything inside me revolted.

Glancing at the recipe, it called for the giblets to be removed from the cavity. Only one problem, I couldn't get the stupid legs apart. Some kind of bar held them together.

What is this, a metal chastity belt for turkeys?

I tugged, yanked, and jerked, for fifteen minutes. Finally, the dark, greasy, cavern yawned open—and I was supposed to put my hand in that?

After stuffing onions and celery in the carcass, and heaving that monster into the oven, I slammed the door shut and leaned against it. This wasn't the way I remembered Thanksgiving at all.

Later that morning, the savory aroma and lively music I remembered from childhood filled the house. The kids were piled on their daddy watching the Macy's Thanksgiving Day Parade while I feverishly worked in the kitchen wearing that blasted rosy glow.

Finally, dinner was served. My husband said grace and then we proceeded to turn into Hoover-mouths. In less than twenty minutes we consumed one hundred dollars worth of food that took two days to prepare.

After dinner, Neal reclined in his chair and the kids ran outside. I was left in a kitchen that looked like Bourbon Street the morning after Mardi Gras.

So this is what my mother did every year?

My hands were chapped. My fingers were cut and burned. Every muscle in my body begged for a glass of wine and a hot bubble bath.

As far as I was concerned, my Mom deserved sainthood.

Glancing out the window, I watched the children jump into a pile of leaves, just like I used to do when I was a child. My husband snored in his easy chair, just like Dad. And I began the arduous task of cleaning, just like Mom.

Indulging in a little self pity, I grumbled under my breath.

Sure, eat all you want and leave the rest to me. Just throw a thank-you over your shoulder before taking a nap.

Nobody had a clue how hard it was cooking Thanksgiving dinner.

Come to think of it, neither did I till now.

Getting off my self-righteous perch, I practiced the true meaning of Thanksgiving. I called my mother and said, "Thank you for all your hard work. We are not worthy of you!"

Write Right

> *I never made a mistake in grammar but one in my life and as soon as I done it I seen it."* —Carl Sandburg

I needed examples to use for chapter three, so I read through a few of my earliest publications and cringed. The only example they could provide is what NOT to do. Even though my first publications were grammatically correct, they were filled with weak writing techniques.

However, a better way to view this is that over the last ten years I have continued to learn and improve. As writers, we should never stop learning and improving our craft.

You may be thinking right now, "But, Linda, you were published even with those glaring weaknesses."

Yes, I was. But in those ten years the publishing world became more competitive. Add that to the shrinking budget for publishing houses and you will realize that in order to be noticed you need an "edge."

In this chapter we will look at the most common mistakes writers make and the techniques that give you the advantage. Notice I wrote "the most common mistakes." There isn't enough room in this book for all the grammar rules. It is advisable that you have several references in your writing library. I've recommended several in the Writers' Resources section in the back of the book.

Words! Keep them simple

Words are what writers are all about. We use them to create images as an artist uses paint. We've already seen how words can change the course of history and the directions of life.

Using them effectively is what births them into the publishing world. Keeping our words simple will actually sharpen our prose.

On several occasions, I've had the opportunity to help beginning writers. One man asked me to read the first chapter of his science fiction novel. The first thing I noticed was his tendency to use "ten dollar" words when "half-dollar" words would have been better. In order to read his manuscript I had to have a Webster's within reach.

I asked him to change them, but he resisted and referred to a well-published mystery writer who did the same thing.

The problem? He wasn't a well-published writer. The same grace isn't given to him. And don't think that by using words like superfluity you are going to encourage your readers to use a dictionary thereby improving their minds.

Did I lose you on superfluity? Did you stop and wonder what it meant? That's another reason to avoid using such words because it pulls your reader out of your story. By the way, superfluity means *overabundance*.

Research has shown that Americans like to read at a sixth-grade level. Why? Well, not because we are dumb, but we are busy. Even in this country that offers an abundance of conveniences we still lose the race with our clocks. We want something we can consume and digest on the run.

Vivid Nouns

Read this sentence:

The bird swooped over my head and landed on the windowsill.

What kind of bird did you see? Let me be more specific:

The Robin swooped over my head and landed on the windowsill.

Do you see how a specific noun creates a sharper mental image? Eating a Porterhouse steak is more interesting than eating dinner. Listening to R&B gives a clearer image than listening to music. Whenever possible, make your nouns specific.

Spark!

Give a specific noun for each of these generic terms:

Actor–
Pie–
Song–
Animal–
Tree–
Drink–
Car–
Sandwich–
Movie–

Keep them active

We all learned in elementary school that verbs show action. The exception to this are the "to be" verbs: am, are, is, was, were, be, become, and became. These verbs show "being" rather than doing. They stop your story from going forward by making the noun motionless.

For instance:

Linda was in the room.

This is a state of being. I am in the room. But what am I doing in that room?

Linda paced in the room. Linda left the room. Linda examined the room.

By using active verbs the sentences were more immediate. They moved forward instead of being static.

Use "to be" verbs when identifying a state of being.

Linda is a writer.

It is also correct to say Linda was happy, but as we discussed earlier, why not write what I'm doing that conveys I'm happy?

Linda danced around her office.

Hmmm, must be good news from my agent.

Adverb Fatigue

Adverbs or "ly" verbs can be tiresome when overused. The first story I sold to Chicken Soup, Mr. Jackson and the Angel Pin, is full of them. In fact, I'm blushing right now. Some of them were necessary, but others could have been eliminated by showing instead of telling.

Here is the story in original form. The adverbs and "if I had it to do over" comments are in bold.

MR. JACKSON AND THE ANGEL PIN

Mr. Jackson wanted to die. He missed his wife who had passed away five months earlier. They had been married sixty-three years and were blessed with five children—children who were busy with their own lives. In his loneliness, he lost the will to live. He shut himself off from the world, quit eating, closed his eyes and waited to die.

Several weeks later he was admitted to the hospital. "Malnourished," the diagnosis reported. During the shift change, the evening nurse **hastily** explained the case to the morning nurse, Freddie. **(During the shift change the evening nurse gave a hasty report to the morning nurse, Freddie.)**

"He hasn't eaten in the two days he's been here," she said **softly. (She lowered her voice, "He hasn't eaten in the two days he's been here.")**

"Hasn't said a word either. He just looks away and

stares off at who knows what. The doc is going to put a feeding tube in his stomach if he doesn't start eating. Good luck, Freddie." With that, the evening nurse hurried out.

Freddie looked at the frail form in the bed. The room was dark except for the soft morning light peeping through the semi-drawn curtain. The white sheets accentuated the outline of his body, which appeared to be nothing more than a skeleton draped with skin. The patient turned his head away and stared at the wall, his eyes void of hope, void of life itself.

Freddie could always find a way into a patient's heart. Somehow she would find a key to unlock his. **Gently** picking up his delicate hand, she held it in hers. **(She took his delicate hand in hers and cradled it.)**

"Mr. Jackson? How about some lotion on your hands, wouldn't that feel good?"

No response. She walked around to the other side of the bed, leaned over and whispered, "Mr. Jackson?"

His eyes widened as he fixed his gaze on the pin she wore—a gold and silver angel given to her for Christmas. **Impulsively,** he reached out to touch it, but drew his hand back. His eyes began to mist and he spoke his first words since being there. "If I had my pants with me, I would give you all the money I have just to touch that pin." **(Impulsively isn't necessary)**

Freddie **quickly** contrived a plan. **(Freddie contrived a plan–it wasn't necessary to say quickly because she made the plan immediately.)** "I'll make a deal with you, Mr. Jackson. I'll give you this pin if you will eat something off every tray we bring you."

"No, Ma'am, I couldn't take it. I just want to touch it. That's the prettiest pin I've ever seen."

"I'll tell you what I'll do, I'll pin it to a pillow and put it next to you. You can keep it until my shift ends, but only if you will eat something off every tray I bring you."

"Yes, Ma'am, I'll do what you say."

When Freddie came to check his lunch tray, she found him **thoughtfully** stroking the pin. **(I'd keep this adverb)** He turned to her and said, "I kept my promise, look." He had eaten a few bites off his tray. They were making progress.

When her shift ended, Freddie dropped in on Mr. Jackson and said, "I'm off for the next two days, but I'll come by here first thing when I get back."

His eyebrows drew together in a small frown, and he lowered his head. Freddie **quickly** added, "I want you to keep this pin and your promise while I'm gone." **(Again, quickly wasn't necessary)**

He brightened a little, but forlornness still hung **heavily** in the room. **(but forlornness smothered the room.)**

"Mr. Jackson, think about all you have to be grateful for—your children and grandchildren, to start with," she encouraged. "Those grandbabies need their grandfather. Why, who else will tell them about their wonderful grandmother?" She patted his hand and hoped for a miracle.

When Freddie returned, "amazing," was the evening nurse's appraisal. Freddie smiled and went to check Mr. Jackson's vitals.

"There's my angel nurse," he **happily** exclaimed. **(A smile spread across his face, "There's my angel nurse.)**

"It sure is, and I've missed you," she replied, noticing the lovely woman who stood next to his bed.

"This is my daughter. She is taking me to live with her," he said. "I'm gonna tell those grandkids of mine story after story." He looked at Freddie and smiled.

"I'm gonna tell them about the angel who took care of their grandpa, too."

Now, Mr. Jackson wanted to live. And live he did, thanks to an angel made of silver and gold, and one made of kindness and mercy.

This is a good story and I think that is why it sold. In fact, it was resold to Woman's World magazine and used by Chicken Soup's internet site. Still, it has a lot of weak writing techniques and writers cannot afford that in today's competitive publishing market.

Raving Repetition

Do you know anyone who constantly repeats a word or phrase? It gets to where that is the only thing we hear, doesn't it? Repeated words in your manuscript are an annoying echo to your reader. The problem is we all have our favorite word to say and to write. I have a lot of them!

The areas to watch for are:

- ***Names***

In a conversation we never repeat someone's name to their face like the example below:

A friend from childhood, Paula, walked toward me. "Hi Linda."

I couldn't believe my eyes. "Hi Paula."

Paula hugged me and said, "Would you like to get coffee soon? We need to catch up."

I smiled at Paula and said, "I would love to. Give me a call."

In our effort to make it clear who is saying what we jar our readers out of the story by constantly repeating names. The remedy for this is after introducing the people at the first of the scene and then use pronouns:

A friend from childhood, Paula, walked toward me. "Hi Linda."

I couldn't believe my eyes. "Hi, Paula."

She hugged me and said, "Would you like to get coffee soon? We need to catch up."

I smiled at her and said, "Sure, I would love to. We really need to catch up. Give me a call."

By writing in "alternating" voices the reader can follow the conversation without repeating the name. If you are writing a story about you and another person in the room the same is true. After introducing that person's name, use pronouns. Don't do this:

Neal and I joined the party. I found a group of gals and Neal found the buffet table. Neal was on his third piece of cheesecake when I brought Cindy to meet him.

Write this:

Neal and I joined the party. I found a group of gals and he found the buffet table. He was on his third piece of cheesecake when I brought Cindy to meet him.

This may seem like a "well, duh, Linda. I know this already." But you would be surprised at how often we make this mistake. It is worth checking after you've finished the article or manuscript.

If a third person of the same gender enters the conversation it is necessary to identify who is speaking by their name, but you can do this in dialogue instead of tags.

Instead of:

Olivia entered the room and Cindy waved. Olivia waved back. Cindy grabbed my hand and we hurried to meet Olivia.

Write this:

Olivia entered the room. Cindy waved and she waved back. "Look, Linda," She grabbed my hand and we hurried to meet her.

- **Words within a sentence or paragraph**

A repeating a word in a sentence or paragraph is the hardest thing to see. Our right brain absolutely does not want to see any error so it puts its hand over our left brain's vision. This is where a good critique group or an honest friend comes in handy. Believe me, Delois found dozens in this manuscript. I thought it was ready to send to the publisher. Thank goodness she caught the things I missed.

Read this sentence:

I picked up the picnic box and walked until I picked out the perfect spot.

Notice the word "pick" is used twice in the sentence and that "picnic" sounds so similar it could be counted as a third. A better way to write it is:

I grasped the picnic box and walked until I found the perfect spot.

There are times that a repeated word is used to emphasis a point. Some words do not offer many alternative choices. In a situation like this be careful when using a Thesaurus to shoot and kill repeated words. It is a handy tool, but don't choose words that are unfamiliar. You could inadvertently change the entire meaning of your text.

If you cannot simply restructure to get rid of repeated words, or find a simple replacement, leave it alone. It is better to repeat than be convoluted.

- **Wordiness**

Using the same word twice isn't the only way we repeat. We sometimes use words that relay the *same meaning* twice. For instance "sit down." How else are we to sit?

The same goes for tuna fish. Tuna is a fish, right? How many times have you heard "free gift?" Excuse me, but isn't *that* the same thing?

Then there is the problem of using two, three, even four words when one will do. Being a southern gal, I am the world's worst offender. I adore the sophisticated sound of, *owing to the fact that.* However one word, *because,* is better. Same for *in order to*—just use *to.*

Check your article or manuscript for these wordy problems.

Tricky Words

Strong inspirational writing keeps the reader "in" the story. As I said earlier, when we use unusual words our reader pulls out of the story and wonders what we are talking about. Another thing that jerks the reader is the wrong use of a word. It is so easy to write *"there"* when we mean *"their"* or *"further"* when we really should use *"farther."* Our spell check doesn't know we really meant "principal" when we wrote "principle," but our reader will.

When I judge a contest and there are two equally great entries I break the tie by choosing the one with *fewer* (not less) errors. Don't be the one who loses because you trusted the spell check feature on your computer.

It is well worth your time and money to purchase a grammar reference book. I've listed several in the Recommended Reading list. Spend some time brushing up on commonly confused words and homophones. Also, refresh your punctuation skills. Know where to use commas, dashes and apostrophes. An omitted or misplaced comma can change the entire meaning of your sentence. For instance:

Let's eat, Granny. Correct.
Let's eat Granny. Very Wrong

Watch your words and grammar. Keep the reader in your story. Don't let anything put a damper on the flame of your inspirational piece.

Homophone Imposters

Our band needs a base guitar player.

This ad sounds good. But what it really says is either, "Our band needs a guitar player who will be our foundation, our fundamental ingredient, or our headquarters." While it is good to have such a person on the team, they may not get what they really need, a *bass* guitar player.

Spell check is a great tool. So great that writers trust it way too much and then the inevitable happens. Therefore, when we write: *The nurse brought in there new baby,* no squiggle line alerts us. After all *there* is spelled correctly.

Homophones, words that sound the same but are spelled different, are especially tricky. When writing we often forget to watch for these pesky word impersonators, but alas, their always there.

Oops, I meant they're always there.

The following list represents the most common errors with brief—not complete—definitions for clarity purposes. I suggest you look these words look up in a dictionary for their full meaning.

aid/aide. Aid is to assist. Aide is the assistant.

all ready, already. All ready is to be ready. Already means by or before a specified time.

all together/altogether. All together is to be all at one place. Altogether means wholly, completely, entirely.

base, bass—Base is the foundation. Bass is low in pitch either vocal or instrumental.

beach, beech—Beach is a sandy shore. Beech is a tree.

broach, brooch—Broach is to bring up a topic. Brooch is a piece of jewelry.

but, butt—But is a conjunction, preposition. Butt is as in "does this make my butt look big?"

capital, capitol—Capital is upper case, or city of governmental seat. Capitol is a building.

canvas, canvass—Canvas is material. Canvass is going door-to-door soliciting votes or polling.

cast, caste—Cast is to throw to the side. Caste is a social class.

censor, sensor—Censor is to forbid. Sensor is an instrument.

coarse, course—Coarse is rough. Course is a plan of study.

complementary, complimentary— Complementary refers to things or people that go together. Complimentary refers to a free bonus gift item or giving someone a compliment.

council, counsel—Council is a committee. Counsel is guidance.

dam, damn—Dam is a structure. Damn is to bring condemnation.

diffuse, defuse—*Diffuse* is to disperse randomly. To *defuse* is to remove the fuse from a bomb.

disburse, disperse—*Disburse* means "to give out," usually funds. *Disperse* means "to scatter."

discreet, discrete.—*Discreet* means showing prudence. *Discrete* means separate, distinct.

douse, dowse–*Douse* is to plunge in water. *Dowse* is to search for water.

dual, duel–*Dual* pertains to "two." *Duel* is a fight to the death.

eminent, imminent, immanent–*Eminent,* originally meaning "emerging", means "illustrious or highly-regarded". *Imminent* means "about to occur". *Immanent,* less common than the other two, means "indwelling, pervading."

exacerbate, exasperate.–*Exacerbate* means "to make worse". *Exasperate* means "to exhaust", usually someone's patience.

flair, flare–*Flair* is a natural ability. *Flare* is to blaze with a sudden burst.

flu, flue–*Flu* is short for influenza. *Flue* is a duct.

hoard, horde.–A *hoard* is a store or accumulation of things. A *horde* is a large group of people.

hale, hail–*Hale* means robust. *Hail* is to call or yell for. Also ice formed in a storm.

holy, wholly–*Holy* means sacred. *Wholly* means completely, entirely.

inherent, inherit.–*Inherent* refers to heredity. *Inherit* is to receive something from someone after their death.

its, it's–*Its* is a possessive pronoun. *It's* is the contraction for it is.

idle, idol–*Idle* refers to lack of action. *Idol* is a person greatly admired.

lead, led–*Lead* is found in a pencil. *Led* is the past tense of lead.

mail, male–These are rather obvious, but I often see one mistakenly used for the other.

mantel, mantle–A *mantel* goes over a fireplace. A *mantle* is a cloak.

meet, mete–To *meet* is to encounter. *Mete* is to distribute.

medal, meddle–A *medal* is a decoration of honor. To *meddle* is to interfere.

moose, mousse–*Moose* is the animal. *Mousse* is the dessert.

naval, navel–*Naval* means seagoing. *Navel* is our belly button.

peal/peel–*Peal* is a chime. We *peel* an orange.

pedal/peddle–We use a *pedal* to propel our bicycles. Salespeople peddle their wares.

principal/principle–A school has a *principal*. *Principle* is a law or standard.

pearl, purl–We find *pearls* in oysters. *Purl* is a knitting term.

reign, rein–*reign* refers to the rule of a monarch. *Reins* are the straps used to control the movements of an animal.

root, route–*Roots* feed plants. *Route* is the path our GPS tells us to travel.

sear, seer–We *sear* our steaks. A *seer* tells our fortune.

stationary, stationery–*Stationary* means fixed. We write on *stationery*.

there, their, they're–*There* is used to describe a location. *Their* is the possessive case of *they*. *There* is the contraction of *they are*.

to, too, two–We all know the difference in these words, but be careful. It is easy to use the wrong one.

Especially the word *too* which means more than needed, or also.

waive, wave–To waive is to put aside, to forego. Wave is what Miss America does from a convertible or a surfer rides in the ocean.

whose, who's–Whose is the possessive of who. Who's is the contraction of who is.

Your, you're–Your is the possessive of you. You're is the contraction of you are.

Beware of these phonies:
Alot
Alright
Irregardless
Theirselves.

The correct usage is:
A lot
All right
Regardless
Themselves.

Punctuation

We writers have a love affair with words and sometimes we do not want to quit our expressive creativity in putting together vivid descriptions, stunning prose, impressive insight, and delightful humor as a demonstration of our talent, our skill in putting words on paper, and really, don't you think this sentence is a little long?

Punctuation is a tool to make our sentences easier to understand. However many writers—especially me—are confused on what to use beyond the period and question mark. A friend of mine who has been on the New York Times Best Seller list many times also admitted to confusion when it came to commas. In keeping with her great sense of humor she once sent her editor a page of commas with a note that she knew they belonged in the manuscript somewhere and instructed her to put them where they belonged.

Again, I will not attempt to cover all punctuation rules, just the ones that give us the most trouble.

- **Apostrophe**
  Forms possessives of nouns.
  Add a **'s** to :
    - nouns that do not end with s *(Linda's)*
    - plural forms of nouns that do not end with s (people's)
    - the end of compound words *(mother-in-law's recipe)*
    - the end last noun to show joint possession of an object *(Neal and Linda's child)*

  Add a **s'** to:
    - Nouns that end with s *(Delois')*
    - plural nouns that end with s *(horses' stalls)*
    - Indicates plurals of lowercase letters *(four b's)*
    - Shows the omission of letters *(shouldn't)*

  Apostrophes also show the omission of letters (shouldn't)

- **Colon**
    - Use between main clauses when the second clause restates or amplifies the first.

  Lilly always wanted to be a novelist: she wrote her first short story at six-years-old.

    - Use after a statement that introduces a list.

  A novelist must practice three things in order to be successful: write, write, and write.

    - Introduces a quotation.

John Donne said: "Reason is our soul's left hand, faith her right."

- **Comma**

> *I have spent most of the day putting in a comma and the rest of the day taking it out.* —Oscar Wild

Use a comma to:
- Separate the elements in a series (three or more things), including the last two that are joined by and, or, or nor. *(He intercepted the pass, ran forty yard, and made a touchdown.)*
- Set off introductory elements. *(Hurrying to work, Carla remembered she forgot to turn off the iron.)*
- Set off additional information that if removed doesn't change the meaning of a sentence. *(The Titanic, which was deemed unsinkable, hit an iceberg and sank in less than three hours.)*
- Connect two independent clauses with a conjunction (and, but, for, nor, yet, or, so). *(He caught the ball, but he fumbled.)*
- When parallel or equal adjectives are used. *(The potatoes had a creamy, buttery consistency.)*

Note: The way to tell if adjectives are parallel is if the word "and" can be placed between them, or if they can be reversed.

- **Ellipsis**

The ellipses is often misused in writing. It is a series of three points with spaces in between them (. . .). Use them to:
- Condense text
    - In the middle of a quotation to indicate the omission of text. Be sure and put a space before and after the ellipses.

- At the end of a quotation to indicate the omission of text. In this case you will use four points—three points and a period. (place a space between the end of the ellipsis and the period.
  - Do not place an ellipsis at the *beginning* of a quotation to indicate an omission of text.
- Convey an unfinished or trailing thought.
- ***Em & En dash***

> **TIP**
> Forming the em and en dash in Microsoft Word: Click on *Insert* above the tool bar, then *Symbol,* click on the *Special Characters* tab. Highlight the Em Dash and click on the *Shortcut Key* button at the bottom. Assign a shortcut key in the box labeled *Press New Shortcut Key.* I assigned *ctrl+m for Em.* Now all I have to do is press *"ctrl and m"* simultaneously. For En I assigned *"ctrl + n."*
>
> In Mac: for en press option, hyphen. For em press option, shift, hyphen.

- The **em** dash is also called a long dash. It is the width of an "m." Some writers put a space between the dash and the word, others do not. However the trend is favoring the spaces.
- The **em** is great to make a thought, information, or a statement stand out. It is especially effective when writing humor or for drama. It also indicates a break in thought or an interruption:

His frustration boiled down to one thing—no time.

- The **en** dash is the width of an "n" and indicates a range of numerals or dates *(200–300)*

- The en dash is not used to indicate a pause or interruption

- ***Exclamation Point***
This punctuation mark is the most abused by beginning writers. The exclamation point is used to convey urgency or strong feeling. It can indicate shouting. However, by using it too often its effectiveness is diluted and actually gets irritating!!!!! Oh, excuse me, I got carried away. Don't use more than one at the end of a sentence

- ***Hyphen***
A hyphen is a short line that has many uses. The most common are:
  - to follow a prefix how–*(how-to)*
  - to follow a suffix–elect *(president-elect)*
  - two words that the writer wants to function as a single adjective *(sticky-sweet)*
  - compound numbers as in *(twenty-one)*
  - when a number, a unit-of- measurement, and an adjective *precede* a noun *(fifty-year-old woman)*
  - However, if the noun precedes the number and unit-of-measurement no hyphen is used *(The woman is fifty years old)*
  - phrases used as adjectives *(unit-of-measurement)*

- ***Semi Colon***
  - Use to join two closely related independent clauses.

  I'm late for work again; this will cost me my job.

  - Use between items in a series.

The planning commission included Harold Gates, president of the arts center; Joan Presley, director of the school for the arts; and Kelly Boyd, the mayor of Preston, SC.

- **Quotation Marks**
  These are used to:
    - Set off direct quotations.

      "Hurry, you don't want to miss this," she said.

      If you have a quote within a quote, use the single quotes.

      "Harriet said to me, 'Peggy, that's the best pie I've ever eaten,'" boasted my aunt.
    - Indicate words used ironically.

      I jumped away from the spider and in my effort to "protect" myself, I broke my leg.
    - For titles of short or minor works, such as songs, short stories, essays, poems, one-act plays, and other literary works that are shorter than a three-act play or a complete book.

Laying Our Words on the Sacrificial Altar

No matter if you are a beginner or a seasoned author, every writer needs to edit. We must take a deep breath and start slicing and dicing, rearranging and rewriting. Following are a few suggestions for this painful process:

- **Get Fresh Eyes**

Put your article or manuscript aside a few days and let your brain rest a few days. You will be surprised at what you find that needs revising. Grab a pencil and highlighter and re-read your piece, correcting and noting all you want to change.

- **Get a Critique**

Even after we revise and edit it is still a great idea to let someone else read our work. The reason is that our right brain doesn't want to see mistakes and will rule out our critical left brain. If you belong to a critique group, or know someone who is honest and qualified to point out any weak areas, let them read it. Even give them a red pen and tell them to have no mercy. Those red marks may be painful, but will actually make your work stronger.

- **Get ready**

After our piece is edited, revised and polished, get it ready to submit. Below is currently the industry standard manuscript form for submitting through the mail.

Use 20 lb white paper.

One inch margins all around.

Either Times New Roman or Courier New font, 12 point.

Double-spaced lines.

A header box on each page (except for the first) with your name, the title of your work, and page number.

On the first page give your contact information—name, address, email address—on the top left side.

On the top right give the word count or in case of a book, page count.

Halfway down the page put the title in all CAPS.

Two spaces down type *by*

Two spaces under that type your name.

Your story should begin two spaces under your by-line.

The first page of each chapter should also start halfway down the page.

If submitting through the mail, do not staple pages together. For articles, mail in a 9 X 12 manila envelope. To send a book-length manuscript you can find a manuscript box at an office store such as Office Depot or Office Max.

Your story—your message, your gift to the reader—is now ready to submit.

Most publishers prefer manuscripts sent electronically and they vary on the form and style. Before you submit, check the particular guidelines of that publisher.

Inspire!

"You are the light of the world. A city set on a hill cannot be hidden. —Jesus Christ

A City on a Hill or a Candle Under a Bowl?

The mountainous task of writing is over. You've edited and polished your manuscript and now it is time to give it wings. But how? Three words: submit, submit, and submit.

You have a story of hope and encouragement, perhaps it is humorous to soothe and heal the weary heart. What are you going to do with it?

In Matthew 5:14 we read about Jesus speaking to his disciples and all who gathered around him. His teaching is known to us as the "Sermon on the Mount."

Here we get a glimpse into the heart of Christ and witness his great love for all people. Even though he is fully aware of the agonizing death he faces on the cross, he is compelled to comfort those who are suffering.

I can almost hear the pleading in his voice as he stresses the importance of reaching out to others and help them as he did.

Jesus reasons that to put a candle under a bowl is ridiculous. We put them on a candle stand so it will give light to those stumbling around in the darkness.

So I ask you, what good are your manuscripts in a drawer and why did you put them there?

Rejection letters

Perhaps you have received the dreaded *rejection letter*. Your writing wings were "clipped" by a faceless editor. That is no reason to hide your light under the bed. There are many reasons for rejections. Usually it is because editors have received many submissions on the same subject, or they may have already published something similar in the past six months.

Maybe your article had some facts wrong. Anyone who is in the publishing business will check your facts to avoid liability. So check your facts first.

Does it have technical problems? I heard an editor who worked for a popular diet magazine. Someone submitted a wonderful article, but misspelled a medical term used in the story. The editor rejected the story on the basis that if the person writing the story didn't take the time to spell medical terms correctly, then how could she trust the rest of the stories claims? Editors do not have time to do our work for us.

Did you send a men's health article to a women's magazine? Again, be sure to study the magazine or publication you plan on submitting to.

And it is possible that your writing didn't jive with that particular editor. So what? There are a lot of publications out there. Submit again, and again, and again.

Tackling Our Writing Demons

Insecurities were my "bowls" that I hid my writing under. I started in my late forties and it seemed that everyone else had been writing as soon as they exited the womb. As the years went by I felt more and more adequate. But I finally *set myself* free from this self-imposed prison. Below is my creative nonfiction article about this experience. If this is your demon, it is my prayer that my experience will be the key that sets you free.

AUTUMN ACHIEVER

Autumn burst on the Ozark hills in dazzling red, orange, and yellow. I thrilled in the colors and crisp fall air while driving to my first writers' conference.

Yes, it was my turn. Me. A middle-aged woman with grown children. My job description had changed from mother and homemaker to fledgling author.

The thrill intensified when I entered the room filled. The energy, the creativity, and the electric buzz of ideas permeated my mind. I chose a table—front and center—and opened my briefcase laden with pens, pencils, highlighters, pads of paper, sticky notes, paper clips, and of course, business cards. The thing had to weigh twenty pounds, but I didn't care because I was a writer.

The room fell quiet when the speaker stepped up to the podium. Pen in hand, poised over paper, I sat at full attention. The first words out of her mouth were, "I've written for as long as I can remember."

Something inside of me flickered. Like a brief power outage. A disturbance in my thrill meter.

The next speaker—who also started writing as an infant—spoke about publishing. He said, "Forget it. Break your pencils. Wad up your paper and throw it in the trash. Go home. All of the opportunities have been filled by people who began their novels long before you middle-aged women finally decided to start."

Well, those may not have been his exact words, but that is what I heard. Smoke curled from where my internal flame had been snuffed out. When I stood to leave the session, my briefcase nearly pulled my arm out of socket.

Old women had no business carrying heavy stuff.

After that weekend, the idea of starting too late haunted me every time I sat at my computer. An evil little publisher sat on one shoulder saying, "It's no use, old woman." But, the desire to put pen to paper sat on the other shoulder asserting, "You must."

I understood why some writers went crazy.

Winter's cold, gray, days reflected my mood. Thank goodness for my critique group. They were the warm fire in my author's hearth. And although we shared in the harsh ice storm of rejection, none of them knew of my self-imposed prison of recrimination for not starting sooner and regretting the time lost. Suffice it to say my motivation took a long winter's nap.

Spring came, nudging the earth to wake up. A friend nudged me by insisting that I give conferences another try and go with her to Oklahoma. I agreed to go, but I traveled light, taking a pencil and pad of paper in my purse. Only writers needed briefcases.

Excitement filled the meeting room as people greeted each other. It reminded me of a family reunion. I chose a table in the back so I could make a quick exit and prepared myself to be reminded—again—that I had started too late and how impossible it was to be published. To my surprise, the speaker began on an upbeat note and asked us to take a few minutes and write a couple of paragraphs about someone who had influenced in our lives.

I wrote about my mother. She'd suffered a hard life, but refused to be a victim. After I left home she decided to pursue her long-time dream of nursing.

As I wrote, it hit me—Mom was middle-aged when she got her GED and went to nursing school. We both pursued our dream at the same age. But, unlike me, she wasn't intimidated that her classmates were in their twenties. The fact that after graduation she had only twenty years before retiring didn't concern her. Why? Because my mother had a purpose.

This revelation jarred my slumbering motivation awake. Exactly why did I write? What was my purpose? Turning to a new sheet of paper, I began to list my reasons: so my children would know their history; to encourage others; to inform; to make people laugh; and finally, for myself.

New direction unfolded in me like the tender leaves of my dogwood tree in April. Determination bloomed in my soul.

Summer's heat intensified and so did my prose. I ignored the evil little editor and only listened to my desire. Finally, he tired of being ignored, so he left to look for someone else's shoulder to perch on.

Autumn, summer's afterglow, brought October and that meant conference time in the Ozarks. While packing to leave, the same thrill coursed through my soul. But this time something was different—me.

Just like autumn, I started writing late in the seasons of life. And like fall, I had a harvest of colorful experiences, collected over many years, to offer my readers. This middle-aged woman, who is living her dream, has something to say.

Remember, it is never too late to inspire.

I'm a Nobody

The book of Psalms is an example of someone writing from the soul. I wonder if David, who is credited for having written seventy-five entries, knew that centuries later billions of people would read his poems, songs, and prayers? Did he expect us to peek into his most vulnerable moments and read his private pleas for his life and the life of his children or his anguished confession for personal failures?

I think he did.

No one saw greatness in this young man who tended sheep on the hillsides of Israel. He wasn't educated in the finest schools and didn't associate with influential people. His companions were sheep. When he rested in the grass, and stared at the clouds, I don't think he ever imagined himself sitting on a throne.

However, during the years spent shepherding, David observed and gathered information about life. He developed his talent for music, learned survival skills, discovered life lessons from nature and most important of all, he drew near to God.

Then came the fateful day when David was brought out of obscurity and crowned king. The boy, David, had the seed of greatness inside him. It grew as he fed it with experiences. Then came the days greatness was birthed on the printed page. And today multitudes are guided, comforted, and blessed by his writings.

Who would have thought it?

We have that same greatness inside us and we are feeding it with life experiences. The day of delivery is different for all of us. If we are faithful to our craft and don't abort, we will give birth.

Who Cares?

You may be thinking, "But, Linda, who cares what I have to say?"

Our future generations care. While writing my novel, I depended on journals, diaries, and letters. The honest experiences and thoughts of people who lived nearly two-hundred years ago added authenticity to my story. The values of those people convicted me to re-evaluate mine. Their courage inspired me.

Unfortunately, every news source today has a spin. Even our school textbooks are fraught with inaccuracies. History is re-written over and over. But if we dedicate ourselves to truth and accuracy in writing about our lives, what we have learned, how we overcame, and our daily walk through life, we will be endowing generations for decades to come a precious inheritance.

It All Counts—My Soapbox

You may not be interested in writing books or being published in magazines. Still, you must write. Keep a journal or a diary. Write letters. It all counts.

Remember Anne Frank's diary? It is read worldwide and provides insight to the turbulent times in which she lived.

My uncle was a WWII veteran. After being diagnosed with terminal cancer, he came to live with me. We thought he had several months to enjoy each other's company, but less than two months after he moved in with us he died. During those precious few days he told me stories about my father who passed away when I was only twelve.

Uncle James also told me about his service in the Second World War. He never saw the value in recording his experiences. Unfortunately, many don't. I listened with relish to his recollections.

Just think, I was with someone who had been there, who had seen what I had studied many years ago in school. Only this time I wasn't reading a text book, I was hearing from someone who had actually served overseas in Germany.

In addition to hearing about WWII, I learned a valuable lesson from my uncle—the importance of "being." One evening after he died, as a way of solace, I wrote about our time together and the lesson I learned.

This is an example of how to use a personal experience to preserve history of everyday life and monumental times in an inspiring way:

THE GIFT OF BEING

I'm a "doer." If you need something done, I'm your gal. My choice to stay at home and raise my five children trained me to multitask, to say yes to everyone who needed help, and to feel guilty when I was doing nothing. For twenty-six years I'd been "doing" for my children, their friends and teachers. My schedule rotated around their schedules.

But now my baby of the family was college bound. Finally, it was my turn—or at least I thought.

One phone call put my freedom plans on hold. The caller said my Uncle James needed me. He had an aggressive form of cancer and experienced complications after surgery. Would I fly to the west coast immediately? I left the next day.

Nothing could have prepared me for the sight of my uncle when I walked into his hospital room. A mere shadow of the man I knew lay in bed, wires and tubes crisscrossing his frail body. He held up his hand. "Hi Honey."

I took his hand and knew that soon my schedule would rotate around his schedule. All week I tried to muster the courage to tell him he could no longer live alone. One evening, our discussion lent itself to broaching the subject.

"Uncle James, what do you think about moving in with us?" I asked.

He considered my suggestion. Since that meant moving to the other side of the country, I knew it would be a big decision. After all, he was an elder in his church, the members were like family, and, more importantly, his beloved wife was buried close by. After a while he nodded. "Yes, Hon, I think I'd better."

After getting him settled in our home, I made it my goal to make sure his last days were pleasant. I barraged him with questions like: Are you hungry? Thirsty? Bored? Do you want to go somewhere? Watch television? Eat? Drink? Do you need anything? Want anything?

He spent his days on the couch watching television programs: golf, fishing, boxing—things that usually bored me comatose. One Sunday afternoon I plopped on the chair next to him while he watched the Buick Invitational.

"My pastime used to be golf," he said. The corner of his mouth turned up and his blue eyes twinkled. "But throwing those irons in the pond got expensive, so I took up fishing."

I chuckled, delighted to see a side of my uncle I never knew existed.

"Watch Tiger," he said. "If he makes this shot, he'll win nearly a million dollars."

Tiger Woods sunk it. Uncle James looked at me and shook his head.

"Poor Tiger, what ever will he do with all that money?"

I stayed with him and watched another tournament. He filled me in on the players, golfing rules and interesting tidbits, like how the grass follows the sun sometimes causing the ball to miss the cup by millimeters. A couple of hours passed, but it seemed like a couple of minutes.

Uncle James reached for his walker and pulled himself up.

"You'll have to excuse me, I've needed to go to the bathroom for quite some time, but put it off because I was afraid you'd leave and start doing something." He shuffled to the hall, stopped and looked back at me. "I've really enjoyed our time together."

An avalanche couldn't have hit me harder. I thought he needed me "doing" for him, isn't that what everyone expects? My uncles simple statement translated in my mind—Stop! Stop what you are doing and take some time being. Be there for others—be there for yourself. Not just physically, but mentally as well. In other words, be where you are—at that moment. Not somewhere else.

That day, I began to practice "being." It wasn't easy. I had to overcome the guilt of allowing myself to do nothing for hours. But, the rewards of those hours will enrich my life forever.

Once, while watching an old war movie, he asked, "Hey, do you have any more of that ice cream?"

"You betcha," I said, jumping up to run into the kitchen. I welcomed any chance to get him to eat. We watched the movie and enjoyed our chocolate chip mint. He turned to me and casually remarked, "I was a gunner for the Air Corps in WW II."

"Really? I had no idea."

He stared off, as if mentally returning to Wurzburg, Germany. "We flew a Douglas A26 attack bomber. She had three fifty-caliber machine guns and a 25 mm cannon."

My interest grew. "Being" was getting easier.

"One time when we were returning from a mission we unloaded our ammo by blowing up haystacks."

"Haystacks?" I grinned. "I heard they were dangerous."

"They were. The Germans hid their weapons under them. And on that particular day when we dropped a bomb on one it exploded. They had a tank under there.

"But the time that frightened me the most is when a fighter appeared out of nowhere and peppered us with bullets. We maneuvered away and escaped. As soon as we landed, I jumped out to inspect the fuselage for bullet holes. One in particular got my attention. It went in one side and out the other." He held his thumb and forefinger slightly apart. "It was half an inch from where I sat. It's a good thing I got religion before I went to Germany." He winked and ate another spoonful.

I didn't want to move. I wanted to spend as much time with this incredibly interesting man as possible.

He told me stories about his experiences with a king from the Middle East, his world-wide travels and his hobbies. One hobby we shared was cooking. I learned this while we watching Emeril Lagasse, one of Food Network's chef hosts. Every time Emeril added spice he yelled, "BAM," and we'd shout "BAM," with him and laugh about our disastrous cooking experiences. I loved "being" with my uncle.

Just before his passing, he lay on the couch and held his hand up, like that day in the hospital. I took it. He thanked me for taking him into my home and for all we'd done for him. I didn't want to let him go. Fifty-five days after moving in with us, he peacefully left this world and went home to his dearly loved wife and his God.

Now, whether listening to my husband tell about his day or visiting with a friend over lunch, whether I'm digging in the dirt with my grandchildren or taking a moment for myself, I'm there—spirit, soul, and body. I'm not making a mental to-do list in my head while I'm supposed to be listening, or playing, or resting. "Being" requires all of me.

It's my turn once again. I'm free to do what I want. But I've changed. Life is a more pleasant journey. Occasionally, when passing that empty couch, I remember Uncle James' lesson. He truly gave the greater gift.

The process of writing was a comfort to me and a valuable exhortation for many, as well as providing a glimpse of WWII from someone who was there.

Write!

Write the rippling circles of life around you. What happens in your home, your city, your state, your country, your world? Do it for our future children, don't put them at the mercy of the news media and the talking heads.

Even if you write a bit of information each day in the tiny square of your calendar, one day someone will read it. I found a book in the Springfield, Missouri library that was published from year's worth of calendars that a woman had kept and saved. She had information about the weather, the price of eggs, and the political news of the time.

Write about your failures, mistakes, trials, disappointments. Tell us how you mustered the strength to overcome. What lessons did you learn?

We have a choice about these shadowy valleys in our lives. Tell how you resisted the temptation to let adversity darken your perspective and instead how it deepened your character.

I wrote earlier that my favorite season is autumn. With one whoosh the air is filled with swirling leaves. They carpet the ground in blazing reds, bright gold, and warm brown. Just because they fell doesn't mean they are no longer needed. They still nurture the tree by incorporating back into the earth providing nutrients for future leaves. *By sharing our lives through the tips of our fingers on our keyboard we strengthen others.*

Write about your triumphs, your successes, the loves in and of your life. Make us smile. Make us laugh out loud till tears stream down our faces. Give us that merry heart medicine.

Write from your soul. Be the hand that reaches through generations to comfort, encourage, and guide.

Inspire!

Printed in the United States
218325BV00001B/13/P